GOD'S LOVE MANUAL

A How-to Guide for Building Successful Relationships

John K Slater

God's Love Manual: A How-to Guide for Building Successful Relationships

Copyright © 2024 John K Slater

Published by: Layman Publishing

ISBN: 979-8-9850912-0-5

No portion of this book may be reproduced in any form, stored in any retrieval system, or transmitted in any form by any means- electronic, mechanical, photocopy, recording, or otherwise without prior written permission from the publisher, except as permitted by U.S. copyright law. All rights reserved. For permissions, contact: www.johnkslater.com

Scripture quotations are taken from the (NASB®) New American Standard Bible®, Copyright © 1960, 1971, 1977, 1995, 2020, by The Lockman Foundation. Used by permission. All rights reserved. www.lockman.org

Scripture quotations marked (NLT®) are taken from the Holy Bible, New Living Translation, copyright ©1996, 2004, 2015 by Tyndale House Foundation. Used by permission of Tyndale House Publishers, Carol Stream, Illinois 60188. All rights reserved. www.tyndale.com/permissions

Disclaimer:

The information presented here does not constitute any form of counseling, health, or medical advice. The information contained in this book is just my personal opinions based on scriptural guidance. Before relying on this information, please seek advice from your professional counselor, healthcare provider, or doctor for your particular concerns.

To my amazing wife, Shelah, for being forever patient as I become the husband God intended me to be.

CONTENTS

1. God's Love Letters — 1
2. A Foundation of Love — 11
3. Kind of Heart — 26
4. I Don't Envy You — 41
5. Humble Pride — 56
6. Dishonor Me Not — 71
7. Eye for an I — 91
8. Mad About You — 108
9. Two Wrongs Too Long — 125
10. What Is Truth? — 143
11. The Armored Connection — 162
12. Trust without Rust — 183
13. I Sure Hope So — 201
14. We're Under Attack — 218
15. Never Surrender — 235

Chapter One

GOD'S LOVE LETTERS

"Scripture remains the lighthouse that defines us, gives us hope, and guides us through life's perilous storms."

Love. It can be a source of so much joy but also of pain and emotional turmoil, frustrating us beyond rationality and tolerance. What causes this contrast of reasoning? Is love a paradox not meant for us to understand? The truth is—we turn love into a wrestling match of personal perceptions and a clash of wills. We complicate love.

Many of our relationship problems are self-inflicted from trying to reshape love into our idealized version of what it should be. As we all know, no matter how hard we try, a round peg cannot fit into a square hole. We must stop forcing what isn't working and shape our behaviors to reflect the attributes of love in the mold as it was designed.

For love to flow in our relationships, we must first comprehend the distinctions in the gender thought processes. By nature, men and women express and respond to love differently. As men, we tend to express our feelings through our actions. We open doors, carry heavy stuff, protect our partners, and run to get the car when it's raining.

Women have a more nurturing temperament, which encourages them to communicate their feelings of love through their emotions. They're inherently more empathetic when we're sick, our hearts or spirits are broken, and often serve as the maternal foundation of the family—the glue. Gracefully, we balance each other out by offering what the other sex lacks or doesn't naturally gravitate toward.

While men and women express love differently, each plays a vital and complementary role in the relationship. A child falling off a bike is a textbook example of how the roles complement one another. While both parents' reactions will focus on the child's well-being, their responses will be inherently gender driven.

When the child falls, both parents rush to assess the severity of any injuries, with the mother leaning toward sympathy and attempting to alleviate any discomfort. The father, on the other hand, will seek to encourage the child to get back on the bicycle as soon as he sees that the child is okay.

The child experiences a mix of gender-expressed love—a perfect balance. They receive security from the mother's nurturing nature and confidence when confronted with a challenge from the father's response. Our example perfectly illustrates how the genders tend to perceive and demonstrate love. When we understand this is how the genders differ in showing affection, we suddenly become more accepting of each other and how we navigate relational challenges.

Our differences help us to strengthen and complement each other's weaknesses, therefore uniting us. We must be careful not to disrupt God's perfectly crafted plan by reshaping how the genders complement and influence the relational structure. God knew exactly what attributes we'd need to assist and support one another. We must trust in His master design for the relationship.

The Dynamics of Love:

God, the ultimate authority on love, provided us with the most effective road map for forging long and rewarding relationships—the Bible. Within its wonderful pages are passages that inspire and encourage love in its intended form that will guide our relationships throughout our lives.

God chose the Apostle Paul, one of the Bible's most notable teachers, to convey the dynamics of love. During his ministry, Paul wrote a letter to the citizens of Corinth, encouraging them to embrace one another by adhering to the key aspects of love. The message from Paul:

> *Love is patient, love is kind. It does not envy, it does not boast, it is not proud. It does not dishonor others, it is not self-seeking, it is not easily angered, it keeps no record of wrongs. Love does not de-*

> *light in evil but rejoices with the truth. It always protects, always trusts, always hopes, always perseveres. Love never fails.* -1 Corinthians 13:4–8 (NIV)

The message within delivers a clear and flawless blueprint for establishing an enduring relationship based on unrestricted devotion. To cultivate our capacity to love, we must first analyze ourselves and recognize our strengths and weaknesses. Why? Because understanding our positive qualities will help us overcome the negative aspects that undermine our relationships.

To begin the transformational process, we must acknowledge that fulfilling relationships don't happen overnight, by chance, or from impulsive behavior. However, all successful relationships harness the understanding of the four essential elements defining love:

- **_Love is_**- *patient, kind*

- **_Love is not_**- *envy, boast, proud, dishonor, self-seeking, easily angered*

- **_Love does_**- *always protects, always trusts, always hopes, always perseveres, rejoices in the truth, never fails*

- **_Loves does not_**- *keeps no records of wrongs, does not delight in evil*

When we break down the passage, we find that there are more suffocating vices than attributes that foster love. Our discovery also indicates that love isn't favored to succeed, but it does reveal its power. Love prevails on the two core building blocks of patience and kindness, that can overcome the detrimental vices that prevent the success of a relationship.

Are you ready to experience love the way God intended? God provided an excellent starting point for learning to love others—our neighbors.

Love Starts with Our Neighbor:

Exodus 20:3-17 found in the Bible's Old Testament, contains God's Ten Commandments given to Moses. The commandments provided structure to the Israelites while also serving as an introduction to the 1 Corinthians passage.

1. You shall have no other gods before me. *(loyalty)*

2. Do not make idols. *(God shouldn't compete with anything in our life.)*

3. Do not take God's name in vain. *(Love does not delight in evil, it is not easily angered, it does not dishonor, love is kind.)*

4. Keep the Sabbath day holy. *(Set aside time for God and our spouse.)*

5. Honor your parents. *(Love does not dishonor.)*

6. You shall not kill. *(We must control our thoughts that*

lead to negative actions.)

7. <u>Do not commit adultery.</u> *(Love does not dishonor.)*

8. <u>Do not steal.</u> *(Love is not self-seeking.)*

9. <u>Do not lie.</u> *(Love always trusts.)*

10. <u>Do not covet.</u> *(Love does not envy.)*

As we can see, the Ten Commandments and Apostle Paul's follow-up message to the Corinthians are linked in how they seek to illustrate love. In the New Testament, Jesus prioritized love for one another as well.

> *"Teacher, which is the great commandment in the Law?" And He said to him, "You shall love the Lord your God with all your heart, and with all your soul, and with all your mind. This is the great and foremost commandment. The second is like it, you shall love your neighbor as yourself. On these two commandments depend the whole Law and the Prophets." (Matthew 22:36–40)*

The uniting component in God's concept of love is that it teaches us to extend to others the same patience, forgiveness, and mercy that He extends to us.

> *So, as those who have been chosen of God, holy and beloved, put on a heart of compassion, kindness, humility, gentleness and patience; bearing with one another, and forgiving each other, whoever has a complaint against anyone; just as the Lord forgave you, so also should you. Beyond all these things put on love, which is the perfect bond of unity. (Colossians 3:12–14)*

The Marriage Commitment:

Marriage is a life-long commitment that can fail if we don't allow God to guide and sustain us along the way. Understanding God's relational design and the need for unwavering devotion to our partners is essential for appreciating the divine marital plan.

> *For this reason a man shall leave his father and his*

> *mother, and be joined to his wife; and they shall become one flesh. (Genesis 2:24)*

Do you notice in the verse above that it says, *"shall become?"* Why? Because a solid marriage entails more than simply exchanging vows and expecting the perfect outcome. It takes time, patience, unconditional love, and steadfast faith in God as He transforms two individuals into one.

When asking several long-term couples what characteristics contributed to their relational success, I received a consistent response—unconditional love. We foster unconditional love by loving someone despite a problem or scenario we may not yet understand. We learn to love through the problems because of our unyielding love for the person.

Just as God is patient with us, we must be patient with one another. We must allow our marriage to blossom according to God's timing and process, not ours. As a result, God's presence will become the relationship's fundamental bonding component and security.

> *And if one can overpower him who is alone, two can resist him. A cord of three strands is not quickly torn apart. (Ecclesiastes 4:12)*

If your relationship needs help, consider this question: Are you committed to its success? There are only two possible responses—*yes* or *no*. Sort of, not sure, and maybe are disengaged replies, falling short of a life-long commitment. Distorted thinking leads to distorted relationships and failure.

> *But let your statement be, 'Yes, yes' or 'No, no'; anything beyond these is of evil. (Matthew 5:37)*

God takes our marital vows seriously, and so should we. If we're devoted to the success of our relationship, God is with us every step of the way. If we allow God to guide our relationships, He promises never to abandon us in our hour of need.

> *And the LORD is the one who is going ahead of you; He will be with you. He will not desert you or abandon you. Do not fear and do not be dismayed. (Deuteronomy 31:8)*

When we trust in God, He loves to show up when least expected and make a way where there appears to be none—He's a way-maker.

A Good Place to Start:

When I chose to write *God's Love Manual: A How-to Guide for Building Successful Relationships*, I composed a set of questions. The questions were designed to reveal how we perceive and experience love and to identify relationship skills that could be improved.

While answering the questions, I realized how much I had grown but also how much I still needed to learn about the simplicity of love. Before we continue, I highly encourage you to ask yourself the same enlightening questions. If you want to examine your relationship's health with the questionnaire, you can download the *Supplemental Relationship Discovery Guide* at:

www.johnkslater.com/newsletter

In the next chapter, our journey begins with patience, vital for cultivating a fulfilling and lasting relationship that can weather life's storms.

Chapter Two

A Foundation of Love

"Patience is the valve that dictates the flow of love from within us into our words and actions."

From childhood, we're taught that waiting patiently teaches us to manage impulsive behavior that can either lead to trouble or a rewarding outcome. This early conditioned conduct becomes our primary relationship resource, fostering a welcoming and understanding disposition within us that strengthens the core elements of love. It becomes the umbrella in the storms.

When relationships fail, it's usually because our tolerance for the other person has been stretched to the limits. In our frustrations, we end the relationship, feeling as if we've hit a dead-end road with nowhere to turn. Before we get to this point, patience can help us negotiate our challenges and avoid the outcome we fear.

With patience at the helm, we're more accepting of each other's imperfections and the problems that can arise from these shortcomings. Patience provides us the time to focus on the issues at hand and resolve them without further damaging the connection.

Numerous insights of wisdom have been written about the value of patience and how it strengthens our interpersonal bonds. Managing our tolerance levels can also help us live longer and more productive lives by reducing excessive tension, which can lead to serious health concerns.

When we consider its importance, it's obvious why patience is such an important quality to cultivate and why it's the first thing Paul mentions when discussing love in his letter to the Corinthians. If patience was the first thing Paul thought of to help people love one another, surely we can see its value in our personal relationships.

From God's Perspective:

Love is—patient

> *with all humility and gentleness, with patience, showing tolerance for one another in love. (Ephesians 4:2)*

From Vice to Virtue:

When I was sixteen, I bought my first vehicle, a 1970 model F-150 Ford truck. It needed several minor repairs and had rust spots and dings in places, but something drew me to it, mainly the price. I spent most of my weekends restoring the truck's body and performing mechanical repairs—but I saw potential. That old truck taught me a few things about automotive repairs—and a valuable life lesson.

As usual, I was working on the truck to fix a problem with the turn signals when a wrench slipped, cutting my hand. The pain caused me to yell at the top of my lungs a curse word that would make a sailor proud. Like a soldier carefully peeking from the safety of his trench, I looked around, hoping my commentary had gone unheard.

All seemed clear, so I returned my focus to the turn signal. Suddenly, my father appeared and asked if I needed help. I gladly accepted his offer. Without further words, we began focusing on diagnosing the electrical problem. While we worked, I couldn't help but wonder whether he'd heard my previous verbal abuse of the English language.

After we finished the repair, he calmly stated, "I would've helped you sooner if you'd asked. I didn't realize you needed help until I heard you yell from across the yard." At this point, I'm still not sure if he heard my full elaboration of obscene remarks. Curiosity got the best of me, and I asked nervously if I was in trouble for my outburst.

"I think you've already punished yourself enough," he said. I was speechless—he was right. By not asking for help, I wasted an entire day, injured myself, and feared punishment for cursing. That day, I learned a life-changing lesson about pride and patience.

As we go through life, we must accept that we may need the help and support of others, and we must communicate our needs. With desire and determination, we can triumph over our pride and develop the patience required to eliminate the behaviors that can be harmful to our relationships.

If we seek to transform our impatient personality into one that will serve us in life, we must rely on what we're trying to achieve—patience. It will take time to work on our ingrained practices. To effectively navigate the challenges of life, we must learn to rely on the following core personality traits:

- Humble

- Good listener

- Considerate

- Relaxed body language

- Positive mindset

- Peacemaker

- Time efficiency

Let's examine the characteristics that add to the relationship's strength. Patience always begins with humbleness.

Humble:

If we were to ask a group of people about the meaning of humility, we'd get various answers. Why? Because the word humble is often misapplied in its context. For clarity, we'll use the biblical definition of humility, which is the absence of pride and arrogance.

An arrogant individual, for example, will focus primarily on their accomplishments, serving to express their superiority. This selfish mindset emphasizes personal views or wants, making conflict resolution with others difficult. We'll never be able to solve a problem until we first discover its root cause. For this reason, we must rid ourselves of the pride that veils us from the truth.

A humble person, on the other hand, readily appreciates the achievements of others and remains receptive to different points of view. They make problem-solving more efficient and beneficial to all parties while leaving us willing to face future problems. Unfortunately, some individuals view humility as a sign of weakness.

Humility isn't a sign of weakness but rather of contentment in valuing and showing respect for others. Humbleness is an essential companion to patience, working together to maintain and strengthen our self-control. Patience allows us to process our thoughts and work through our obstacles effectively, transforming them into beneficial actions.

The strength of humbleness unites us and changes the "all about me" mindset into an "it's all about us" approach—a winning formula for successful relationships. We now have the prerequisites for becoming a good listener.

Good Listener:

Now that we've committed to improving our patience and humility, we need to round out our team with the good listener quality. This skill is acquired by the acknowledgment that we may go into a conflict without truly knowing the problem. We cannot read minds and must never assume, leaving us with no choice but to listen humbly and intently to understand where the other person is coming from. By doing so, we avoid hearing only what we want to hear and can promptly begin to resolve the true issue. A skilled listener also employs one crucial key to achieving clarity in communication—timing.

The primary rule of good listening is to refrain from having talks when all parties cannot focus. Before initiating a conversation with someone, try to determine their present demeanor. This initial assessment of a person's emotional state often saves time for all parties. Distracted thoughts tend to impair communication.

Consider this: would you attempt to hold a serious conversation with a football fanatic during the Super Bowl? The person may try to pause the game and listen out of respect, but chances are they'll only pay half attention to the talk.

What about the exhausted partner who has worked six straight days and just got home from a twelve-hour workday? Would they be capable of giving us their full attention? Understandably, their primary focus would only be on food, a shower, and a good night's sleep.

When the timing is off, communication may be misconstrued, worsening the situation. If everyone doesn't appear to be in a state that permits them to focus on the topic, postpone the discussion. Patience increases our listening skills, allowing us to reach successful solutions while demonstrating consideration for others.

> *This you know, my beloved brethren. But everyone must be quick to hear, slow to speak and slow to anger. (James 1:19)*

Considerate:

So far, we've discussed how patience and humility will help us become better listeners by taking into account the feelings of others. We can further develop our patience by learning to be considerate in all aspects of our lives.

For example, allowing someone to go ahead of us in the grocery checkout line or helping a sick neighbor shows consideration. In many ways, being thoughtful of others is about sharing our time. As youths, we learn this by raising our hands and waiting to contribute to class discussions. Love begins to flow like an inviting brook when we patiently consider the feelings of others.

However, if not nurtured, our managed tolerance and regard for others can deteriorate as we mature How can this happen? As adults, our everyday responsibilities compete with our available free time. Our time is occupied by our families, friends, careers, and goals, forcing us to fight for a moment to ourselves.

To continue to be thoughtful of others, we must be mindful of our need for personal time. When we exclusively think about the needs of others, resentment can fester in our hearts. We all need time to focus on ourselves without feeling guilty or letting anyone try to make us feel like we're being selfish. If we spend most of our time focusing on others and someone doesn't understand our need for time as individuals, they should reconsider who's being selfish.

The simplest way to cope with resentment developing over a lack of personal time is to encourage "me time" in the relationship. Make it a habit to let those in our lives know that time to ourselves is important to us. This approach reduces animosity and fosters consideration for the other person, as well as relational balance and unity. Making time for ourselves allows us to reflect on who we are as individuals, promoting a relaxed personality that will be receptive to everyone in our lives.

> *In everything, therefore, treat people the same way you want them to treat you, for this is the Law and the Prophets. (Matthew 7:12)*

Relaxed Body Language:

I've always considered body language the "language of mixed emotions." Why? Because the flailing hands we see when someone is overjoyed might also mimic the flailing hands of a troubled person. I arrived at this conclusion because I'm a visual learner, having experienced this confusion. I naturally communicate my ideas or emotions to others through gestures, but to help avoid any miscommunication, I try to minimize my body language.

If we're a person that often uses physical gestures to express our thoughts or emotions, there are three key points to consider:

1. When calm, we employ less bodily motions.

2. Exercise caution when discussing difficult or sensitive topics. Body language might be misinterpreted as adversity.

3. Visual learners tend to express themselves unconsciously through body motions.

When interacting with others, it's important to minimize body language to avoid giving the mistaken impression of frustration and potentially escalating the situation. If we do feel we're becoming frustrated during our interactions, we should pause until we can calm down. Taking short breaks will allow us to unwind and return to the conversation with an optimistic outlook. Again, patience saves us from aggravating circumstances by attempting a resolution while frustrated.

After we have our body language under control, the person we're communicating with will be less likely to be confused by our body gestures, and effective problem resolution will be possible. We can now continue the discussion with a positive mindset.

Positive Mindset:

It's probably safe to say that if we just won a million dollars, we'd be more open to the challenge of solving a complex or potentially frustrating problem. The contentment of our good fortune would surely make us more willing and tolerable of an issue than during a time of tragedy. That's just how life works, and we must harness that reality as a resource of knowledge.

For example, what if we just lost our job? Unlike good fortune, losing our source of income would likely induce stress, cause our brains to work erratically, and increase negativity. We should postpone important decisions or discussions until we relax, knowing that we're unlikely to reach an acceptable solution and how difficult it will be to remain hopeful during this period.

Unfortunately, we cannot always avoid engaging with others during less favorable moments. In such instances, we must learn to patiently filter our words and actions. Remember, positive thoughts yield positive results—and peace.

> *Watch over your heart with all diligence, For from it flow the springs of life. (Proverbs 4:23)*

Peacemaker:

In some sense, everyone desires peace. Although, is peace even feasible in a culture where people clash over such trivial differences? Is it even conceivable for our relationships to achieve a state of harmony and unification? Yes, humanity is capable of harmony with one another—it all starts with a decision.

> *If possible, so far as it depends on you, be at peace with all people. (Romans 12:18)*

We cannot control others, but we can choose to live in peace, which can help influence others to do the same. To encourage others, we must embrace the most honored attribute of a patient person—the peacemaker.

The peacemaker employs humility, attentive listening, a considerate nature, calm gestures, and optimism to foster harmonious relationships. When there's a problem, they minimize the negative, accentuate the positive, or opt not to engage. They understand how our emotions might influence our decisions and actions during life's difficult times, using this knowledge to sustain peace.

They may choose not to engage in the resolution of an issue since, in some cases, exercising patience and letting matters resolve themselves is the best and only course of action. Sometimes, we may be tempted to try and resolve a situation, but it's always wise to "let go and let God" address the problem for the best results.

> *with all humility and gentleness, with patience, bearing with one another in love,*

> *being diligent to keep the unity of the Spirit in the bond of peace. (Ephesians 4:2–3)*

Time Efficiency:

While everyday commitments take up a large portion of our time, we must still spend quality time with our partners and set aside time for ourselves—it's a must. Managing our schedule is the simplest and most efficient way to ensure we devote quality time to our relationship. We'll find it easier to maintain patience if we learn to manage our time.

> *Therefore be careful how you walk, not as unwise men but as wise, making the most of your time, because the days are evil. So then do not be foolish, but understand what the will of the Lord is. (Ephesians 5:15–17)*

Final Thoughts:

To improve patience, I practice two strategies. My favorite acts like a brake—PPD.

Pause (Stop and filter your thoughts.)

Process (Process your actions or words.)

Deliver (Use constructive words or actions.)

The second method is placing myself in situations that demand patience. For example, practice driving along a busy street during rush hour or shopping at Walmart during peak hours. It may appear to be self-inflicted agony, yet it works.

Exposing ourselves to situations that test our patience teaches us to control our tolerance levels for our environment. Patience is a powerful relational resource and can change the most challenging circumstances, even when we think it's hopeless. It's the most effective free resource we can harness that will improve the potential of having a successful relationship, capable of withstanding whatever life unfolds.

I've heard it said that time is the one thing we can't buy more of—patience contradicts that philosophy. Patience allows us time to correct behaviors that a proud nature will consume. So, when you think about it, patience is the token that will buy time for us to become the person our partners need and desire.

It's the building block of relationships—the key to success in all we do.

Strategy for Success:

- Always be humble through contentment.
- Practice shared listening and speaking.
- Calm body language helps others relax.

- Choose to be the peacemaker.

- Time management helps control our patience.

- Always practice being considerate to others.

- Some situations require "letting go and letting God."

Related Scripture:

- *Romans 12:12*

- *Proverbs 15:18*

- *Ephesians 4:2*

- *Romans 8:25*

- *Philippians 4:6*

Let God Fight the Battle:

*Heavenly Father,
We ask that You strengthen our patience in all aspects of our lives.
As we learn to love others as we love ourselves, may*

we demonstrate to others the compassion You graciously grant to us.

We pray for patience while waiting for Your perfect plan to unfold in our lives, knowing that You'll never abandon us.

Give us a patient heart, mind, and spirit as You bring our marriage together as one to serve You.

In the name of Jesus, we ask these things,
Amen.

Chapter Three

Kind of Heart

"Kindness can change a moment, but it can also change us if practiced consistently."

On a hot summer day, there's nothing more refreshing than a glass of ice-cold sweet tea with a slice of lemon. Throughout the years, I've tried to acquire a taste for unsweetened tea, the healthy version, but after many failed attempts, I gave up. Tea just isn't the same enticing beverage without that indispensable touch of sugar. In the same respect, our relationships can always benefit from a similar sweetener—kindness.

One of my earlier flaws, which most likely contributed to failed relationships, was my lack of showing others acts of compassion. It wasn't that I didn't see the point in being considerate to others or that I was a mean-spirited person—kindness was just an inconvenience.

As a young man trying to conquer the world, I was too busy being a full-time student and working to support a family. In those days, not much help was offered to ease the burden. Government agencies seemed to support those unwilling to help themselves and disregard those who needed a little temporary help. I suppose not much has changed in that way of thinking.

My parents would've gladly helped me with my early struggles, but they both passed when I was a young adult. I was pretty much on my own to figure things out. Finding a way to make it all work boosted my confidence, but it also made me bitter, which I passed on to others.

My views on education began to reflect a lack of sympathy for individuals unwilling to make the sacrifices or devote the time required to advance in life. I reasoned that if I could do it alone, others could, and everything else was merely an excuse.

The negativity that had become a part of me continued manifesting in every corner of my life. When someone was in need, and I had the knowledge to help, my first thought was always, "What have they done to help themselves?" I avoided the situation if possible. For years, this thought process would become my solution for what I considered laziness.

After all, everyone has twenty-four hours a day to be productive or a life anchor for others. While there's some truth in that statement, it doesn't come with any sweetener to encourage or inspire others. A better approach to life is to find out what a person needs and to add the splash of kindness that builds relationships—"How can I help?" Now, that's the good stuff.

Those early years taught me that we must let go of the things that make us bitter and add a splash of kindness to make life sweet for ourselves and those around us. If we seek a kind-hearted nature that bonds us to others, we must rid ourselves of pride, selfishness, and a sense of entitlement. All it takes is a little faith in God and one another, some effort, topped with a dash of kindness.

> *She opens her mouth in wisdom, And the teaching of kindness is on her tongue. (Proverbs 31:26)*

From God's Perspective:

Love is—*kind*

> *For by these He has granted to us His precious promises, so that by them you may become partakers of the divine nature, having escaped the corruption that is in the world by lust. Now for this reason also, applying all diligence, in your faith supply moral excellence, and in your moral excellence, knowledge, and in your knowledge, self-control, and in your self-control, perseverance, and in your perseverance, godliness, and in your godliness, brotherly*

> *kindness, and in your brotherly kindness, love. (2 Peter 1:4–7)*

From Vice to Virtue:

Through the years, I've learned to be more sensitive to the needs of others, but I'm still working on not being too busy. As a result of my cancer treatment, I'm learning to slow down and realize that the world doesn't have to be conquered in a single day and enjoy life's journey. After all, we only have one life, and we better take advantage of what we've been given. This is it—no do-overs.

Ironically, I thank God for my cancer, which has taught me so much about life. Most importantly, it has taught me to make time for others, as well as time for myself to relax and appreciate God's creation. My motivation for starting to write was to perhaps use my lifelong blunders to help others as a way of giving back. I can't give you doctorate-level advice, but I can tell you what I've learned from years of making mistakes.

Along life's journey, I've found that loving people have characteristics geared toward supporting others. Their nature is contagious and calming, encouraging us to emulate their selfless compassion. They'll typically exhibit the following distinctive characteristics, the examples for which we should all strive for:

- Giving

- Sincerity

- Positive

- Gratitude

- Forgiving

With effort and practice, we can cultivate the characteristics mentioned above, but first, we must understand why they may be missing in our personality. As a new office manager, I recall an exhausting but memorable day that made me pause and consider how our rushed lifestyles influenced our display of kindness. It began one day when I was pressed for time, as usual.

It was a rainy day, causing me to leave for work later than usual, and I found myself racing to make up for the delay. To make up more lost time, I tried organizing papers while driving and accidentally spilled my coffee. The coffee ruined several forms I needed for my morning meeting. At this point, my emotions were churning.

I arrive at work, park, and rush inside, hoping to recover some of my coffee-soaked documents before the meeting. I'm greeted at the door by news of a broken printer and other typical office problems. In my frustration, I began issuing commands for everyone to deal with the situation, like the adults I hired. Later, I even refused a day off for an associate who needed to attend to family matters.

When I got home and was winding down, I reflected on my inconsiderate attitude earlier that day. My initial concern was, am I a terrible person to work for? After some thought, I realized I'd have to ask those who worked with me. The next day, I began asking everyone how they felt, assuring them there would be no consequences for their opinions.

Most of our work team had been together for almost a decade, so they were comfortable talking to me about nearly anything. After talking with the team individually, I received my answer. Everyone agreed, "I was always rushed, which made me all business and sometimes inconsiderate."

With an open mind, I accepted the verdict of why they'd reached their conclusion about my personality. Setting my pride aside, I realized they were right. I was always too preoccupied with my objectives to stop and consider the feelings of others.

I had neglected to be an advocate for compassion while focusing on my selfish ambitions of being an awesome new office manager. In hindsight, I should've spent more time validating my team's needs and showing genuine concern about what was going on in their lives.

Until that point, I held the belief to give my all to whatever I did—to benefit me. It's an awesome concept; however, if we fail to encompass others in the concept of that meaning, it becomes a selfish approach to life. In other words, we should strive to be the best person we can be while supporting others.

In future interactions, I began filtering the three primary offenders that can obstruct successful communication and consideration for others. I remembered the method by using the acronym TWA:

- **T**houghts *(Am I feeling negative emotions?)*

- **W**ords *(Will my words be constructive?)*

- **A**ctions *(Will my actions help the situation?)*

Let's look at the three filters in the TWA acronym and how they can help us maintain self-control and foster kindness.

Thoughts:

On more than one occasion, I've let my emotions run wild and said or did something I later regretted. In retrospect, I'd ask myself, "What was I thinking?" Over time, I understood that I was continuing to put myself in regrettable situations by failing to regulate my emotions. FYI—I still make mistakes; they're a work in progress.

Everything we say or do, whether beneficial or detrimental, originates from our thought process. To effectively connect with people, we must learn to regulate our reactions, or the unpleasant emotions we allow to fester in our minds will manifest as negative words or behaviors. We either sow positive communication seeds that create the intended outcome or ones that can hurt our objectives.

For example, would there be a profit if we opened a savings account but failed to contribute money? Although the money seed was planted, the savings account was neglected, resulting in the only possible outcome—failure. In comparison, when we engage with others, we must start by planting a positive seed and nurturing it to fruition.

When engaging with others, we also unconsciously plant an expectation of an outcome in our minds. Why? Because of our ingrained upbringing and life experiences, we've formed a perception of how things should or shouldn't be done. Therefore, for success during communication, we must balance our desires and validate the other person's expectations.

We must learn to find an acceptable compromise between two distinct individuals who are the result of conditioned learning from the mold into which we were born and reared. Essentially, we uncover the other person's needs and fill them with a reasonable compromise for both parties—a balance. We've now combined our compromising thoughts with our positive remarks to reach the goal of our interaction.

> *Do not be deceived, God is not mocked; for whatever a person sows, this he will also reap. For the one who sows to his own flesh will reap destruction from the flesh, but the one who sows to the Spirit will reap eternal life from the Spirit. (Galatians 6:7–8)*

Words:

Our words are the second TWA filter and the most severe way to cause emotional distress or shatter someone's confidence. Our spoken words can also inspire one another to greatness, encourage us through the most difficult of challenges, and comfort us beyond measure, leaving us with a choice. A choice that is to be made wisely.

> *Death and life are in the power of the tongue, And those who love it will eat its fruit. (Proverbs 18:21)*

Our unfiltered emotions are irrevocable and can significantly impact the relationship's stability. Words can cut deep and take time to heal, even after forgiveness has occurred. If our partner has forgiven us for our hurtful remarks, there's still the fear of recurrence or whether we truly meant them. We must be careful not to let our hurtful words define us.

> *But the things that proceed out of the mouth come from the heart, and those defile the man. (Matthew 15:18)*

We must also avoid employing a harsh tone when attempting to communicate. A harsh tone is similar to adding an adjective to a noun—it describes something about the subject. Harshness possibly represents a disgruntled person, quickly putting an end to our aspirations for a productive conversation session. A pleasant and kind attitude will always yield more favorable results than irritated comments.

If we fail to manage our negative thoughts, harsh tone, or unfiltered remarks, we allow the situation to escalate into bad behavior, intensifying the problem we're trying to resolve.

> *He who restrains his words has knowledge, and he who has a cool spirit is a man of understanding. (Proverbs 17:27)*

Actions:

The final filter in the TWA acronym is action. Once we reach this point of negativity, we've caused relational damage that will continue to surface, making the situation difficult to mend. To avoid this frustration point, we must consistently practice filtering our thoughts and words. How can we practice filtering our emotions without being in conflict with our partner? Every morning at the start of a new day, we can discover an opportunity to practice.

On a regular basis, our workplace offers us the opportunity to hone our skills in sorting our emotions. The work environment is usually diverse regarding personalities, preferences, time restrictions, rules we must adhere to, and personal objectives. The likelihood of disagreements increases in this type of environment that demands our self-control, lending us the perfect school for learning to control our wayward thoughts.

Strangers also provide us with opportunities to develop kindness. Do we stop to aid someone having car difficulty, give our resources when a need is presented, or help someone struggling with their arms full? Every day, there are numerous chances to practice kindness. What do we do with the opportunities? Do we use them to serve others while helping us become better people?

Change can only occur by application—we must practice showing kindness until it becomes a habit. Through our efforts and patience, we'll gain control over the detrimental actions that escalate conflict and produce destructive behaviors.

> *He who pursues righteousness and loyalty finds life, righteousness and honor. (Proverbs 21:21)*

Final Thoughts:

Because of our intense feelings, we may sometimes feel compelled to lash out at others. But will losing control of our emotions help or only serve to aggravate the situation? When our emotions are vulnerable, we must remember to use the TWA thought filtering method. During our moments of weakness, when we may lose control, TWA acts as a peacemaker and referee.

Before addressing an emotional subject with someone, we must first recognize the difficulties we may face. Our greatest challenge will be pride, which can manifest in all of us. If pride is powerful enough to cause Satan to lose his prestige role in heaven, it can easily cause us to fail in communication or showing kindness.

Pride will utilize denial, such as, "I don't have a problem with harsh words!" Then, if we add deflection to the equation, "Why are you accusing me of a harsh tone when you never listen to me." Suddenly, defensive mode shows itself, "Maybe if you would listen and try to understand me, I wouldn't have to use a harsh tone to get your attention."

The communication disconnects highlighted above present possibilities for us to improve and become more productive problem solvers. I can't begin to count the time I've let my emotions take over the conversation and it becomes a wasted venture for all parties. Nothing we think, say, or do out of kindness will ever achieve the results we seek when dealing with others.

If we don't believe we have a communication problem, yet we still struggle to communicate, perhaps our pride is concealing the truth. Yes, our partner may be a contributing factor, but if we address ourselves, half of the problem will disappear. The half we have accountability for is within our control.

In time, and with some effort, when we cultivate compassion in ourselves, it will permeate into our relationships. Whatever difficulties our relationship faces, when kindness becomes our nature, our hearts will overflow with words of patience and love capable of overcoming any challenge. The dynamics of a successful relationship that we've been striving for will begin to emerge and will be within our grasp.

> *The good man out of the good treasure of his heart brings forth what is good; and the evil man out of the evil trea-*

> *sure brings forth what is evil; for his mouth speaks from that which fills his heart. (Luke 6:45)*

Strategy for Success:

- Use the TWA method to filter any potential negative thoughts, words, and actions.

- Plant the good seeds of a kind heart.

- Discuss any thoughts, words, or actions with our partners that need forgiveness. *(Discuss—Resolve—Forgive—Heal)*

- Practice complimenting others.

- Remember, kindness benefits both the recipient and the giver.

- Don't expect our kindness to others to be returned. Kindness is about who we are, not who others need to be.

Related Scripture:

- *Matthew 5:40–43*

- *Luke 6:27*

- *Galatians 5:13*

- *Luke 6:35*

- *Matthew 7:12*

Let God Fight the Battle:

Father,
Give us the strength and understanding to carry forth Your goodness in all we do. Help us recognize the needs of others when opportunities to show love present themselves, expecting nothing in return. We ask that Your example of compassion, gentleness, and generosity be the example we show the world.
May the goodwill You instill in us continue to inspire future generations as our hearts are guided by patience.
Show us how to bring You honor through our thoughts,

words, and actions in all things.
May we always be willing to forgive others as You forgive us.
In Your holy name, we ask these things,
Amen.

Chapter Four

I DON'T ENVY YOU

"Envy erodes our conviction of being blessed by God and diminishes faith in Him knowing what's best."

Some of my earliest and most cherished memories are of my family's Tellico Plains, Tennessee, farm. Our 150-acre property bordered the Tellico River, which hosted our summertime swimming, hiking, and fishing activities on countless occasions.

There were fields of corn stretching as far as the eye could see, with an old tobacco barn near the edge of the field, which acted as a fort for our imaginative young minds. Next to the barn was an old automobile that had found its final resting place under an apple tree, lending itself as the getaway car for playing cops and robbers. In between our imaginary shootouts, the tasty apples offered a quick snack before the sunset finally called the day to our adventures.

Unfortunately, we were forced to sell the farm that created so many fond memories due to my father's health issues. As my father's health declined, he retired early, and we relocated to Florida and lived on a tighter budget in the years that followed. Moving away from the farm marked the beginning of my struggles with envy. Despite our financial predicament, I still wanted to do all the things I saw other kids doing. I was suddenly a child who had to sort out everything out of the norm in my life.

It was difficult at times to accept all of the things I felt I was missing out on. Sometimes, it felt impossible. Through the years, my parents rarely tossed a ball around or joined me in any activities I was involved with growing up. With my parents being elderly and my father being sick, it limited their involvement in most of my life. This lack of attention, which forced understanding, persisted as I grew older.

To compensate for the loss of family income, my father began buying houses and restoring them with my grandfather, forcing us to relocate constantly. I was always going to a different school and making new friends. At times, I felt it would be easier to wear a name tag and save my classmates the trouble of learning this kid's name.

The constant relocation wasn't as bad as the embarrassment I felt living in some of the older dwellings we refurbished. My envious nature that had developed deep within became a justification for lying to make myself feel better about my life. In an attempt to feel normal, I began lying about anything that seemed out of place to make me seem normal.

At a young age, I made do with many things out of necessity and gave up some things I felt I deserved. As an adult, I can see how someone can unintentionally develop an envious approach to life, believing they're entitled to what others may take for granted.

Later, as we become adults, this entitlement mindset infuses into our personality, infiltrating our relationships and causing problems. In reality, we must learn to be content with the lives we've been given and to recognize what holds real value and importance. It's not the fast car we drive, the two-story house we live in, or the designer clothes we wear.

It's about spending time with family and waking up to the love of your life that you rush home to embrace. It's having that special relationship that can openly talk about anything—a safe place to land. It's about having the assurance that our partners have our back no matter what we confront in life. That's the good stuff, the stuff that matters.

> *Not that I speak from need, for I have learned to be content in whatever circumstances I am. I know how to get along with little, and I also know how to live in prosperity; in any and every circumstance I have learned the secret of being filled and going hungry, both of having abundance and suffering need. (Philippians 4:11–12)*

While envy is commonly associated with a desire for material belongings, it can also be directed at a person's lifestyle, marriage, family, qualities, career, or prominent status. If it's a person, place, or thing, as humans, we've envied it at some point in our lives. I've envied all of these things and have seen the troubles they can cause in a relationship.

Before proceeding, let's take a moment and define the difference between envy and jealousy. Envy and jealousy have similar implications, yet they differ in their expression. Envy is our desire for something that belongs to someone else, while jealousy is our fear of someone taking what belongs to us.

Allowing envious thoughts to manifest will often lead to physical actions, changes in routine, or perspectives that can be detrimental to our relationships. The fall of Lucifer, the angel God created to be superior, was the first documented instance of pride and envy working in tandem, leading to disastrous outcomes.

> *"Son of man, take up a lamentation over the king of Tyre and say to him, Thus says the Lord God, "You had the seal of perfection in beauty. You were in Eden, the garden of God; Every precious stone was your covering: the ruby, the topaz and the diamond; the beryl, the onyx and the jasper; the Lapis*

> *lazuli, the turquoise and the emerald; and the gold, the workmanship of your settings and sockets, was in you. On the day that you were created they were prepared. "You were the anointed cherub who covers, And I placed you there. You were on the holy mountain of God; you walked in the midst of the stones of fire. You were blameless in your ways from the day you were created until unrighteousness was found in you. (Ezekiel 28:12–15)*

God had blessed Satan, but he desired more despite his many superior qualities and astounding beauty. Satan selfishly became envious of God's position, seeking to rise above his creator in status. After Satan persuaded many of heaven's angels to follow him, God removed them from heaven.

> *But you said in your heart, I will ascend to heaven; I will raise my throne above the stars of God, and I will sit on the mount of assembly in the recesses of the north. I will*

> *ascend above the heights of the clouds; I will make myself like the most high. (Isaiah 14:13–14)*

Another devious act of envy was committed by Cain, Adam and Eve's firstborn son. The story unfolds with Cain and his younger brother, Abel, presenting sacrifices to God. Cain, a farmer, gave a variety of his harvest as an offering, and Abel, a shepherd, the very best of his flock.

God favored Abel's sacrifice, and Cain became envious of his brother's offering, killing him and becoming the first recorded murderer. Envy—became a catalyst for murder.

> *Then the LORD said to Cain, "Why are you angry? And why has your countenance fallen? "If you do well, will not your countenance be lifted up? And if you do not do well, sin is crouching at the door; and its desire is for you, but you must master it." Cain told Abel his brother. And it came about when they were in the field, that Cain rose up against Abel his brother and killed him. (Genesis 4:6–8)*

As God indicated in the above passage, we must learn to conquer our envious thoughts, which create negative and often regrettable results. Envy is a powerful emotion that can destroy relationships and must be overcome.

From God's Perspective:

Love does not—*envy*

> *For where jealousy and selfish ambition exist, there is disorder and every evil thing. (James 3:16)*

From Vice to Virtue:

Imagine strolling down the banks of a rippling brook on a warm spring day, watching the flowers adorning the banks extend their magnificence of beauty to the rising sun. As the trees dance to a gentle wind, birds wake and arouse our ears as they sing their morning lullabies. We smile with our eyes as the tiny hummingbirds hover above the flower buds, collecting their morning reward. We feel at one with nature.

For the moment, there's unity and peace in our world. Why? Because the brook, the flowers, nor the birds are envious of anything belonging to the other. There are no inferiority complexes or threatening feelings, only the joy of nature coexisting as one.

If we can learn to let go of our envious and self-centered desires, we'll be able to appreciate each other's differences and how they enrich our relationships. Without insecurities, we'd no longer feel inferior to others and could exist in harmony, as does nature.

A relationship afflicted by insecurities and discontentment will be one of neediness, with one spouse striving to control the other. The good news is that envious tendencies can be overcome—first, we must find the root cause of the emotions. The following personality flaws are indicative of an envious nature:

- Finds fault in others

- Takes credit for others' ideas

- Exaggerates about themselves

- Cannot contain gossip

Finds Fault in Others:

An envious person will often make self-serving remarks to downplay our accomplishments while justifying their lack of achievement. When I was seventeen, I had a friend who was a never-ending fault-finder. He was quick to say, "Not bad, but I can do better." Everything felt like a competition—it became nauseating.

Growing tired of feeding his ego, we eventually drifted apart as friends. I later discovered that his parents rarely complimented or encouraged him, creating the need to rely on his friends for approval.

If we're not complimented or encouraged as children, we'll continue to seek excessive acceptance from others as adults. The intense desire for approval can drive us to interrupt discussions to praise ourselves or dismiss the accomplishments of others. Envy doesn't share the spotlight.

> *These are grumblers, finding fault, following after their own lusts; they speak arrogantly, flattering people for the sake of gaining an advantage. (Jude 1:16)*

Takes Credit for Others' Ideas:

We labor long hours on a tedious assignment, only to have someone take credit for our hard work—it's infuriating. It can leave us feeling violated and less likely to collaborate with others on future projects. We could voice our frustration, but that wouldn't change the situation.

Rather than voicing our frustration, we could approach the perpetrator, letting them know they've misrepresented our work, which has disrespected us and is unethical. Nevertheless, we're willing to help them improve or learn any skills necessary to deliver original work.

Approaching the person in this manner achieves two objectives. First, it informs them that we know they're claiming credit for our work. Second, it allows the development of their competencies rather than relying on stealing someone else's work, breaking the cycle. Last but not least, we kept our composure and conveyed kindness when it wasn't easy—we grew from the experience.

Rather than focusing on being the victim, we exhibited leadership by assisting a teammate, potentially stopping an envious disposition from developing further.

> *He who walks in integrity walks securely, but he who perverts his ways will be found out. (Proverbs 10:9)*

Exaggerates about Themselves:

Most of us have probably overstated the facts about ourselves at some point to impress someone or make something more appealing—as I slowly raise my hand in agreement. The problem with deception is that it tends to lead to further deceit to keep the truth hidden. It can become a never-ending cycle of coverups.

To escape the cycle of embellishing reality, we must look deep within ourselves and rewire our belief that we're entitled to more and that our life is lacking. Never again should we think that God made an error with any part of our being—He doesn't make mistakes. We're an amazing person, just as He created us.

We'll never feel at ease or comprehend God's incredible blessings for our lives unless we allow our true selves to exist in a contented state of existence. Only after imprisoning the envious monster that has infiltrated our lives will we experience unselfish love as God intended. We must embrace the masterpiece that God created us to be.

> *For we are God's masterpiece. He has created us anew in Christ Jesus, so we can do the good things he planned for us long ago. (Ephesians 2:10)*

Cannot Contain Gossip:

Patsy Davis, my mother-in-law, once told me, "I'll remember what you say long after you forget about it." If we follow that advice, we'll save ourselves a lot of heartaches. Before spreading gossip or rumors, we should consider the potential long-term impact it could produce.

We must feel comfortable communicating within our relationships without fear of the topics becoming public domain, which requires trust. Gossiping can diminish or destroy that mutual trust, creating boundaries that make solving relational issues difficult.

The envious personality that seeks self-centered objectives often serves as the core motivation for gossiping. As the perpetrators of gossip, we fail to follow Jesus' instruction to love our neighbor as ourselves. Who would purposefully reveal insensitive, harmful, or destructive information about themselves?

Always address problems discreetly and avoid the corrosive whispering that can undermine the faith and security of our relationship. Don't let the whispers of gossip serve the objectives of envy and weaken our partner's trust.

> *Argue your case with your neighbor, And do not reveal the secret of another, Or he who hears it will reproach you, And the evil report about you will not pass away. (Proverbs 25:9–10)*

Final Thoughts:

Years ago, as Christmas approached, I persuaded a friend to join me at a volunteer event to help those in need. When I arrived at his house to pick him up, he rushed to the car, jumped in, and commented about the chilly weather. We were Florida natives, so anything below forty degrees was freezing.

I suppose the coldness in the air inspired his next remark, "It's freezing—the less fortunate should get a job so we can relax on our day off." The following conversation topic was about his desire for a new, high-end, expensive smartphone. I acknowledged with a constrained, silent nod, not knowing what to say.

We arrived at the volunteer event, asked the hosts how we could help, and were directed to our designated area to serve. Our host had asked us to hand out various items as each person passed our table. As they made their way through the line, we gave each an item of food, clothing, toiletries, and other items. You could feel their immense gratitude and joy—it was just a toothbrush or a can of soup, but for them, it was an answer to prayers.

On the way home, my friend appeared deep in thought, staring straight ahead at the road. I asked him what he thought of volunteering, and he replied, "It was a good feeling. I liked it. You know, I guess I can get a few more years out of my phone. It still makes calls." I turned to look at him and smiled as he expressed his new perspective on needs versus wants.

My friend had found contentment like an inviting spring day, a gently rippling brook, birds singing their morning lullabies, and flowers offering only a peaceful beauty without contention or a sense of competition. As with nature, we must be at one with one another, without jealousy or discontent, finding our treasure in one another.

When we allow envy to control our lives, we spend precious time chasing what doesn't matter. We should be content with what we have, or we may miss out on the beauty that surrounds us and the immense blessings from God that we already possess. We each have been given a unique divine role to help one another, not compete for what the other person has.

Let the love of God and our partner always be enough and the focus of our time—love does not envy.

> *For where your treasure is,*
> *there your heart will also be.*
> *(Luke 12:34)*

Strategy for Success:

- The primary cause of envy is resentment of others' accomplishments.

- Let what God blesses us with always be enough.

- We must learn to be content with the one-of-a-kind person that God designed us to be.

- Establish goals. They contribute to removing the urge to be envious of others' achievements.

- Rather than accepting credit for others' efforts, learn what's required to develop our abilities to create original work.

- Recognize others' successes and express an interest during conversations by asking questions and providing positive feedback and support.

- Let any gossip end at our ears.

Related Scripture:

- *James 3:16*

- *James 4:2–3*

- *James 3:14–15*

- *Proverbs 14:30*

- *Proverbs 27:4*

Let God Fight the Battle:

Dear Lord,
At Your feet, I lay my envious nature.
Please help me be content with myself and the person you created me to be.
Help me understand and accept Your divine plan for my life, knowing You provide all my needs.
Search my heart for any misdirected desires in my personality that I need to address.
In the name of Jesus, the name above all others, we humbly ask these things,
Amen.

Chapter Five

Humble Pride

"When the lion's roar is laden with too much pride, God will send a tiny thorn of humility to hush the mighty beast."

I will always be amazed by how God works and the timing in which He does so. During the time that writing this book was merely a vague thought churning in my mind, I remember a conversation with Shelah. It happened early one morning as we drove to the airport to fly to Branson, Missouri, for vacation.

To pass the time on long rides, we usually throw topics of interest into the air, pluck one, and talk about it until it leads to another. That morning, the first topic was how my early family history resulted in some strained relationships. Shelah, trying to be helpful, suggested that there might be some unresolved issues from my past. Feeling as if Shelah thought my prior handling of the past was inadequate, I responded agitatedly, "Can we please not talk about my past? I just want to relax."

My sudden comment triggered a cold in the air, accompanying us on the foggy early morning trip. At the time, I wasn't sure why I became frustrated with Shelah, but it deserved some thought since it had happened before over the same issue. I reflected on the conversation with Shelah and addressed the topic with my counselor, which led me to recognize she was right—there were unresolved past issues.

For years, pride had closed my eyes to the truth. After many sessions with my counselor, I finally put the issues haunting me to rest. Looking back, I'm thankful Shelah persisted in talking about the unresolved issues of my past. It was because of her persistence that my pride weakened, and I recognized, addressed, and discussed my past failures—with you. Going forward, my writing incorporated more of a nakedness about me that, at first, I was reluctant to share.

Pride is the most powerful enemy we'll ever confront. It hides in the shadows, concealing our full potential as individuals and undermining the unity and well-being of our relationships. While we can never totally eliminate pride, we can raise awareness of its constant presence and reduce its negative consequences.

As with any vice, we must first learn how to combat our foe. Let's dig in, soldiers.

From God's Perspective:

Love does not—*boast*—*it is not proud*

> *Boast no more so very proudly, do not let arrogance come out of your mouth; for the Lord is a God of knowledge, and with Him actions are weighed. (1 Samuel 2:3)*

From Vice to Virtue:

Every victory in our lives has God's fingerprints, and we want to give Him the spotlight, not ourselves. Words like "self-made" and "self-reliance" are egotistical terms and should be removed from our vocabulary. Why? Because the "self" words insinuate God's disengagement from our lives and His sovereign will for us.

One of my favorite teachings of Jesus that highlighted humanity's humble and prideful nature is the Pharisee and the Tax Collector parable. It's a simple warning about the perils of allowing our pride to govern us and how it can close our eyes to reality.

> *Two men went up into the temple to pray, one a Pharisee and the other a tax collector. The Pharisee stood and was praying this to himself: God, I thank You that I am not like other people: swindlers, un-*

just, adulterers, or even like this tax collector. I fast twice a week; I pay tithes of all that I get. But the tax collector, standing some distance away, was even unwilling to lift up his eyes to heaven, but was beating his breast, saying, God, be merciful to me, the sinner! I tell you, this man went to his house justified rather than the other; for everyone who exalts himself will be humbled, but he who humbles himself will be exalted." (Luke 18:10–14)

From Our Perspective:

Once upon a time, a couple madly in love had their first fight. The conflict lasted all night, the next day, and a week that grew into a month. After a year, someone finally asked the couple what had sparked such an unending dispute between the once-loving couple. After much deliberation, neither person could recall how the quarrel began, only that it wasn't their fault. The made-up story of the arguing couple serves as a reminder of how we can waste precious moments allowing pride to control our thoughts.

We all wish we had more time, yet, like sand, we carelessly let it slip through our fingertips. To overcome egotistical personality traits, we must identify and eliminate the characteristics that generate pride:

- Egotistical
- Loathes advice or instructions
- Loathes personal criticism
- Self-centered
- Self-admiration
- Desire to control situations

Egotistical:

EGO—a tiny three letter word with the power to do much harm to ourselves and our relationships. I have always said a fitting acronym for ego would be:

*E*xcessively *G*oing *O*verboard—of thinking too highly of ourselves.

Most definitions of the ego are negative, focusing on pride and arrogance, but is having an ego always a bad thing? When we think of having an ego, we typically imagine it as a negative trait to overcome. Interestingly, we all have egos that help us build confidence—and developing confidence is a vital aspect of life as it helps us achieve our objectives.

The issue emerges when a positive ego becomes arrogant, creating a toxic atmosphere for ourselves and those around us. Arrogance makes it difficult to admit shortcomings, attain goals, admit a lack of understanding, or accept counsel. Why? Because acceptance of any character deficiency is a show of weakness for the egoistic personality.

With an inflated self-image, advice is perceived as a waste of time, pointless, and even insulting, making accepting responsibility difficult—admitting to being the reason for relational conflict is unlikely. If we wish to interact effectively with people, pride is never a good character trait to have. A relationship hampered by an egoistic personality will always experience limited progress.

> *When pride comes, then comes dishonor; But with the humble there is wisdom. (Proverbs 11:2)*

Loathes Instructions from Others:

On a rushed trip to South Florida that got off to a late start, I tried to find a detour around the nerve-racking Florida Turnpike. If you've ever driven this toll road, you understand why I wanted to avoid the fast pace associated with the multiple exits, which you only notice when the GPS suddenly tells you to exit.

Shelah had proposed pulling over and using our cell phones to find alternate routes, but I assured her I knew the way. It appears that not asking for directions is a male ego condition linked to our conquering nature—thus, I ignored her advice. With my manly confidence, we began our detour around the turnpike. It went something like this:

After assuring Shelah I had a plan, I took the proposed detour to our destination. As we drove down the highway, we began to settle back and enjoy the beautiful sunny day and the God-painted scenery. Suddenly, nothing on the road ahead looks familiar. I began wrestling with whether I should continue, turn around, or maybe research the route, as Shelah mentioned.

For a brief moment, I ponder asking Shelah for help, but the words "I have this" resurface in my mind leaving deep gashes in my damaged ego. A lump forms in my throat as I realize, "I don't have this. I think we're lost." The next thing to enter my mind—I will have to swallow my pride and tell her we're lost!

When our ego is left in charge, we tend to become closed-minded and unwilling to accept guidance. We need to learn to trust what our spouses often bring to the table. Remember, we don't know all things about everything—we need each other. On that humbling day, an insightful and beautiful message penetrated my heart.

> *Two are better than one because they have a good return for their labor. For if either of them falls, the one will lift up his companion. But woe to the one who falls when there is not another to lift him up.*

> *Furthermore, if two lie down together they keep warm, but how can one be warm alone? And if one can overpower him who is alone, two can resist him. A cord of three strands is not quickly torn apart. (Ecclesiastes 4:9–12)*

Loathes Personal Criticism:

Pride not only prevents us from proactively accepting guidance but also constructive criticism. For example, Shelah, being a meticulous veteran schoolteacher, typically proofreads my writing for grammar and clarity. As valuable as her keen regard for detail is, it's not always easy for me to accept her suggestions.

The first time I asked her to proofread part of a manuscript, I expected her to find several errors. Surprisingly, she returned it with a smile and assured me everything was okay. I was shocked but pleased with my efforts as I rushed off to begin another chapter. However, I wasn't prepared for the next proofreading session.

As prideful as a puffed-up blowfish, I expected another smiley face of approval. Instead, she began scribbling notes—everywhere—lots of them. The notations continued as she read, pausing only to give her quick opinion on certain parts. I was slowly becoming irritated by her extensive editing when she handed it back to me.

In my egocentric opinion, the chapter was decently written. Of course, I removed myself from my lengthy torture session with my self-proclaimed masterpiece before allowing her to share her thoughts any further. As I began reviewing her notes, I started to feel terrible. The notations she had made, in all fairness, clarified the message in the chapter.

I had let my pride overlook her sincere honesty, meant only to help my writing come together. I later apologized for my ungrateful attitude, attempting to explain how my pride had gotten the better of me.

> *The way of a fool is right in his own eyes, But a person who listens to advice is wise. (Proverbs 12:15)*

Self-centered:

God designed us with an ingrained self-preservation to help us stay focused while maintaining our spiritual and physical well-being. The issue with this built-in behavior is that if unchecked, we can cross the line between its constructive goal and allowing self-centered conduct to emerge.

Our natural preservation can be demonstrated by an infant crying to be fed, changed, or held—all of which are needed. However, when children get older, and we satisfy their unwarranted desires due to crying or pouting, self-centeredness emerges in their developing personalities.

A new mother once informed me that she always bought her daughter a toy when shopping to avoid her crying. "Do you think buying a toy whenever you enter a store is wise?" I asked, thinking this was unusual.

"I don't want her to grow up wanting things like I did. I'm going to give her everything I can," she said.

I thought to myself, while this mom means well, she may come to regret her current way of thinking. As her child grew older, she became more insistent on being the center of attention, demanding her way and sulking when challenged.

If this type of conditioned conduct is not addressed, it will develop into one-sided relationships later on in life. It will be the only natural response she knows and how she interacts with others. Remember, life isn't all about our needs and desires—if the emphasis is always on us, we must adjust our mindset.

> *One who separates himself seeks his own desire; He quarrels against all sound wisdom. (Proverbs 18:1)*

Self-admiration:

America's thriving financial culture promotes an endless accumulation of wealth and recognition to fuel our egotistical triumphs. In this type of social environment, self-admiration can give rise to seeking undeserved praise and feeling entitled to selected lifestyles. While we all need, appreciate, and enjoy praise, we should never seek unwarranted attention or flaunt our accomplishments—let others have that job.

One of the most effective things I've done to curb self-admiration was to remove all achievements displayed on social media or the walls of my home. This new perspective allowed me to see less of myself and more of God and the worth of others in my life, something I had previously overlooked. If we don't humble ourselves, God will humble us.

> *Because of the privilege and authority God has given me, I give each of you this warning: Don't think you are better than you really are. Be honest in your evaluation of yourselves, measuring yourselves by the faith God has given us. (Romans 12:3)*

Desire to Control Situations:

During my career, I've worked with many diverse people who were amazing at problem-solving. They all shared one common bond—they love to brainstorm with others and listen to understand, not just respond. By exchanging ideas, we avoid neglecting potential concerns, shorten the time required to attain results and increase the potential for sustainable and lasting solutions.

When we share ideas as a team, we share leadership, removing any single person from controlling the situation. Because of the loss of dominance, an egotistical personality struggles to thrive in this form of integrated idea-sharing. They quickly express their disdain by constantly nitpicking and prolonging the process with their superior vision of the best possible outcome.

This need to control situations typically develops over time and can, initially, be motivated by factors other than pride. For instance, a person suffering from obsessive-compulsive disorder, or OCD, may have uncontrollable thoughts and behaviors. They may be overly concerned with keeping things perfect or in place—acting on the compulsions that control them.

Childhood experiences can also influence a desire to exert control over situations. If a person grows up experiencing numerous lifestyle changes or overbearing parents, it could contribute to a need for control as a form of emotional protection.

If a dominant personality is motivated by something other than pride, we must learn to be understanding and supportive while we try to help them overcome their challenge. Small, shared projects are an excellent place to start. Maybe paint a room together while they concentrate on the walls and you on the ceiling, or vice versa. While painting the room, practice refraining from commenting on how they could do the wall better—be content with their result.

As you work, ask them if they see anything we missed or could improve. It makes no difference if their work has defects or if they made a mess while painting. Our goal is to demonstrate that both team members can offer suggestions as well as accept them.

It's about trying to help them remove prideful tendencies and the need to control situations—it's about the relationship.

> *Therefore if there is any encouragement in Christ, if any consolation of love, if any fellowship of the Spirit, if any affection and compassion, make my joy complete by being of the same mind, maintaining the same love, united in spirit, intent on one purpose. Do nothing from selfishness or empty conceit, but with humility consider one another as more important than yourselves; do not merely look out for your own personal interests, but also for the interests of others. (Philippians 2:1–4)*

Final Thoughts:

Pride is the vice that will lure us into a false sense of security by diverting our attention away from character flaws that we should address or change. When pride is no longer a hindrance, we'll begin to see progress in overcoming what we formerly felt were insurmountable obstacles. We can begin to develop the rewarding and satisfying connection we desire once we've overcome our pride—the wrecking ball of love.

Strategy for Success:

- Reduce pride by complimenting others, removing the attention from ourselves.

- We all have something to offer—find it in others as well as ourselves. Convert arrogance to humility.

- Once a day, tell our spouse one thing that they're good at or that we rely upon.

- Once a week, ask our spouse one thing we could improve in our relationship.

- Always consider constructive "criticism" as personal "construction."

- Volunteering encourages us to divert our attention away from ourselves by meeting the needs of others.

Related Scripture:

- *Proverbs 11:2*

- *Proverbs 16:18*

- *Proverbs 27:2*

- *1 John 2:16*

- *Galatians 6:3*

Let God Fight the Battle:

Precious Lord,
Replace our prideful heart with humility that nurtures lasting relationships.
Lord, may our tongues only speak words that will encourage and inspire others.
Let us always humble ourselves before our Creator in all aspects of our lives.
We pray for a humbleness that will saturate us and flow over into the lives of others.
In the name of our merciful savior, Jesus Christ,
Amen.

Chapter Six
DISHONOR ME NOT

"Disrespect is like tossing a stone into calm water. It causes ripples to travel outward, upsetting what was once a serene environment."

In this chapter, we examine four root offenses that jeopardize and devalue our partners, preventing us from having the relationship we seek. There are many ways to bring dishonor to a relationship, but the four we'll explore can have serious and long-term implications. First, let's raise awareness of these four horsemen of a toxic relationship: pride, selfishness, anger, and dishonor.

They're a skilled quartet of mayhem-makers who enjoy using our thoughts, words, and actions as weapons to inflict damage and undermine relationships. As previously mentioned, the tongue can inflict tremendous pain on our victims due to its fast delivery, unexpectedness, and relentless use. Our tongue has the power to inflict such deep pain that it can take years to heal, if not impossible, to forgive.

> *Now if we put the bits into the horses' mouths so that they will obey us, we direct their entire body as well. Look at the ships also, though they are so great and are driven by strong winds, are still directed by a very small rudder wherever the inclination of the pilot desires. So also the tongue is a small part of the body, and yet it boasts of great things. See how great a forest is set aflame by such a small fire! And the tongue is a fire, the very world of iniquity; the tongue is set among our members as that which defiles the entire body, and sets on fire the course of our life, and is set on fire by hell. (James 3:3–6)*

Aside from the tongue, Galatians reveals the most prevalent practices we must learn to control to respect ourselves and others. All of the following are behaviors that originate from pride, selfishness, anger, and dishonor:

> *Now the deeds of the flesh are evident, which are: immorality, impurity, sensuality, idolatry, sorcery, enmities, strife, jealousy, outbursts of anger, disputes, dissensions, factions, envying, drunkenness, carousing, and things like these, of which I forewarn you, just as I have forewarned you, that those who practice such things will not inherit the kingdom of God. (Galatians 5:19-21)*

We must search our hearts to discover if any fleshly desires need to be addressed in our relationship. If our relationship suffers from the detrimental behaviors described in the Galatians' message, we must prioritize restoring the connection with our partners. To do so, we must be willing to discuss any topic, accept any accountability, and assure them we're willing to make the necessary effort to change the behavior.

Go slow—when the relationship has been damaged, there will be hurt that may warrant difficult conversations, mutual understanding, and time to forgive and heal—patience.

From God's Perspective:

Love does not—*dishonor*

> *Be devoted to one another in brotherly love; give preference to one another in honor. (Romans 12:10)*

From Vice to Virtue:

Now that we've explored some of the offenses detrimental to the relationship, let's look at what we can do to promote unity and to change our dire circumstances—the fruit of the Spirit:

> *But the fruit of the Spirit is love, joy, peace, patience, kindness, goodness, faithfulness, gentleness, self-control; against such things there is no law. (Galatians 5:22–23)*

As we can see, the fruit of the Spirit contributes to the positive qualities of our relationship by building on the basic elements of love (<u>love is</u>: *patient and kind*). These favorable characteristics will continue to endear us to our spouses and bring honor to all aspects of our relationship.

First and foremost, each partner must respect each other for the individual that God created. We accomplish this by recognizing the worth of our partners and letting the fruit of the

Spirit guide our thoughts, words, and actions, honoring the bond between us. The four primary areas in which we disrespect and devalue others, motivated by pride, selfishness, rage, and dishonor, are:

- Moral issues
- Positions of authority
- Individualism
- Sexual immorality

Moral Issues:

Relationships must be built on morals that instill confidence in our partners, knowing we'll always do the right thing—even when no one is watching. Years ago, I recall seeing a commercial where a child observes a parent using drugs. One day, the parent notices the child getting high and asks where they'd learned to use drugs. "I learned it from you," the child replied.

I'll never forget that commercial and its lesson of setting a good example for those around us. Even when we don't think anyone is watching, doing what's right will ensure we make a habit of retaining our partner's honor.

The integrity of the upright will guide them, but the crookedness of the treacherous

> *will destroy them. (Proverbs 11:3)*

Positions of Authority:

We've all probably heard phrases like, "I've had someone tell me what to do my entire life." I won't let anyone boss me around anymore!" The statement obviously implies that the problem with listening to authority stems from someone in their past.

As a young manager, I recall a coworker who often seemed irritated when I assigned them tasks. One day, as usual, they appeared to be having a problem with something I had asked them to do. Exhausted by the constant pushback, I asked why it was always such a struggle when I asked them to do something.

"Why do you always want me to do it? It's not like I'm the only person that works here," they quickly replied. I responded by saying that I understood their concerns but relied on their help in completing specific tasks for which they were skilled. I also conveyed my appreciation and asked if they were interested in training someone to help in the future.

After our conversation, I could tell they felt appreciated, especially now that they had the opportunity to train someone. Our problem solved itself through unifying leadership instead of forcing them to endure with a "boss mentality."

During our conversation, they opened up and explained why they reacted harshly to my assignment requests. I discovered they'd endured an abusive childhood and a controlling partner in a previous relationship.

Always take the time to understand what someone is feeling, which shapes their emotional reactions, by showing compassion and, most importantly, patience. I'm glad I chose to respect them while feeling disrespected. Sometimes, we have to first show others what we seek and are willing to give.

> *Every person is to be in subjection to the governing authorities. For there is no authority except from God, and those which exist are established by God. Therefore whoever resists authority has opposed the ordinance of God; and they will receive condemnation upon themselves. (Romans 13:1-2)*

Individualism:

This is one area where we can really complicate the relationship—and ourselves. I've tried to change others to my liking and had them try to change me, and neither will work. It's like standing barefoot in an army of mad ants—it won't be tolerated long.

God knew what He was doing when making us. He knew we wouldn't complement our differences if we were all alike. A relationship, as God intended, consists of two people who maintain their individuality while establishing a union. As they unite, the positive and negative aspects of each individual blend, improving the relationship—a balance.

Our relational conflicts are triggered mainly by the clash of our differences as they come together. Ever wonder why mature couples have fewer conflicts? Through the years, they've overcome their pride and accepted their partner's individuality, appreciating what they each bring to the team. They've learned to work out their differences while being different.

When disagreements arise within our personalities, we compromise until reaching a solution involving two distinct individuals—a simple answer to an often complex dilemma. When we try to change our partners, the change rarely lasts, and we end up causing friction in the relationship—we stand in an army of mad ants.

> *Now I urge you, brothers and sisters, by the name of our Lord Jesus Christ, that you all agree and that there be no divisions among you, but that you be made complete in the same mind and in the same judgment. (1 Corinthians 1:10)*

Sexual Immorality:

Sexual infidelity is probably the most challenging of the disrespectful offenses to overcome, leaving the victim suffering from severe emotional pain. As a young and ignorant man, I regrettably caused someone heartbreak by viewing pornography—a type of infidelity. I'll never forget the pain I saw in the eyes of the person I hurt.

At the time, I tried to justify my actions by convincing myself that viewing adult material wasn't the same as physically committing adultery—not true. I reasoned that my lust was solely directed at someone on a digital screen, and I would never cheat in reality. Still, their pain remained, as if they'd been physically harmed inside, so my argument lost its strength.

When I devoted my life to Christ, I realized the full depth of my error. Although the lust that drives the act isn't with a flesh and blood person, it remains a form of infidelity with the potential to hurt our partners.

> *"You have heard that it was said, 'YOU SHALL NOT COMMIT ADULTERY,' but I say to you that everyone who looks at a woman with lust for her has already committed adultery with her in his heart."*
> *(Matthew 5:27–28)*

Pornographic content is easily accessible in today's technological world. It's everywhere, infiltrating every part of our lives.

It has become a social scourge, degrading the gift of intimacy, which God intended to be shared only by married couples.

It has no compassion for the poor, our gender, race, or age, or makes any attempt to avoid the life of a faithful Christian. It destroys all that entertains its influence. To defeat and repel the monster, we must first understand how it creates a stronghold in our lives. We start with this passage found in Corinthians:

> *The wife does not have authority over her own body, but the husband does; and likewise also the husband does not have authority over his own body, but the wife does. Stop depriving one another, except by agreement for a time, so that you may devote yourselves to prayer, and come together again so that Satan will not tempt you because of your lack of self-control. (1 Corinthians 7:4–5)*

First, let's be clear, the passage doesn't imply that we can assault each other sexually at any given time. Its objective was to clarify two extreme sexual concerns widespread in the newly founded Corinth church, which can also help modern-day couples when its wisdom is applied.

One group in the church believed that married couples abstaining from sexual activity would become more spiritual Christians. Another group thought it was acceptable to engage in incest, fornication, and prostitution—a concept derived from the common practice of worshiping their temple gods.

Paul resolves the opposing matters by conditionally combining them—leaving out incest and prostitution. He clarified that married couples shouldn't limit their intimacy and should fulfill each other's needs. Why? Because we can open the door to temptation if we fail to maintain sexual relations with our spouses.

To compound the problem further, intimacy became a sort of bargaining weapon. Have we ever withheld intimacy as a bargaining tool to get our way or as retaliation? This demeaning behavior can complicate problems and lead to even greater relationship issues. If this is happening in our relationship, we must end the no-win practice.

I'm not suggesting we pursue intimacy during moments of conflict or when our emotions are suffering from a problem that needs resolving—I'm saying we should resolve the issue so the union can resume intimacy. An unsolved issue that closes the door to intimacy can lead to temptation. Scripture warns us:

> *Be angry and yet do not sin;*
> *do not let the sun go down*
> *on your anger, and do not*
> *give the devil an opportunity.*
> *(Ephesians 4:26–27)*

If there are any relational conflicts causing us to distance ourselves from our partners, we must express our feelings and work toward reconciliation and forgiveness. Even while dying on the cross, Jesus forgave His executioners. Can our hearts be so bitter that we refuse to forgive our loved ones if Jesus could forgive His executioners while dying?

> *But Jesus was saying, "Father forgive them; for they do not know what they are doing." And they cast lots, dividing up His garments among themselves. (Luke 23:34)*

We must let yesterday's problems fade into the past, live in the present, and look forward to tomorrow. We must overcome our pride and offer forgiveness, removing any potential for Satan to plant seeds of temptation.

We often judge individuals for turning to pornography or adultery while ignoring the root causes of their sinful behavior. While the perpetrator bears responsibility, we may share some blame for their falling victim to temptation. That may not be what we want to hear, but it's what we need to hear.

We may argue the point, "I didn't force them to get on the computer and look at that filth!" While this statement is true, do we also consider it beneficial to withhold intimacy for almost a year or use it as a tool to get our way? We must always consider how our actions might impact one another.

Please understand that I'm not offering any justifications or pointing the finger at anyone else but the person committing the sexual immorality. They're entirely accountable for their choices. Still, we must accept responsibility for withholding affection and allowing the devil to have a stronghold in our relationship.

Relationship concerns that cause us to withhold our affection must be addressed. No excuses—if we can find time to browse pornography, retaliate for misconduct, or get our way, we can find time to talk with our partners. While discussing sexual matters in a relationship can be challenging, it's necessary. Remember, during discovery sessions with partners, the goal is to find solutions to our lack of passion, not to cast blame.

If we believe our lives have become monotonous due to routine, our excitement for romance can fade—in which case, we must express this to our partner. The foremost indication that our alone time with our spouse has become dull is that we know exactly how the evening will unfold during the experience.

If this is the case, begin to introduce fresh ideas and desires to break up the monotony and revive the romance—never stop dating. You might discover that you've both been hesitant to suggest a shared desire, resulting in "I never knew you felt that way!" followed by a wink and grin.

Another point to consider is "Remember who loves you!" When we're sick or in need, it's not a picture on our computer, cell phone, or magazine that comforts us. It's the person we wake up beside and fall asleep with every night—flesh and blood—a person with real feelings that we can hurt with our actions.

> *I will set no worthless thing before my eyes; I hate the work of those who fall away; It shall not fasten its grip on me. (Psalm 101:3)*

Pattern of Disrespect:

We've all shown disrespect in some way at some point in our lives. It happens—like spilling milk. All we can do is, clean it up, apologize, and move on. But what if disrespect becomes a habit? We can't keep ignoring it, hoping it will go away—it will probably only worsen if we do, causing us to lash out in frustration. When this happens, we put the relationship on a cycle of offense-forgive-offense-forgive pattern that pushes us apart.

> *Do not be deceived: "Bad company corrupts good morals." (1 Corinthians 15:33)*

To break the repetitive cycle of conflict, we must have those difficult conversations that lead to resolution. Remember, avoid starting the conversation with anything that could cause defensiveness, such as, "You make me angry when you disrespect me!" Never begin an unpleasant discussion while standing in an army of mad ants.

Always initiate conversations with something like, "I've been feeling irritated with our relationship lately and want to see if we can fix it." A sweetener added to a potentially bitter situation. This not only helps prevent defensiveness, but it also holds us accountable for managing our emotions. Point of consideration, nobody makes us feel anything—we allow our emotions to control us.

After we begin the conversation—keep it on topic. It's natural to want to vent as the opportunity presents itself, but try to avoid frustrated ranting about everything at once. It becomes counterproductive and can cause us to lose our grip on our emotions, rarely resolving the underlying problem. If this happens, the conversation will usually end where it started—in frustration.

Another point—don't try to resolve in-depth issues in one session. It always does more damage than good. Conflict resolution could be compared to a boiling pot of water. The longer the water boils, the hotter it becomes—much like the long hours of heated disputes.

Limit the conversation to one topic and one hour. Long chats can test our patience, resulting in frustration—fruitless sessions that yield no results. We must learn to pace ourselves and allow the natural problem-solving process to breathe.

Sometimes We Need Boundaries:

Wisdom—we must first respect ourselves before expecting others to do likewise. Recognizing our worth as individuals is half the battle in confronting disrespect. God created us in His image, complete with our appearance, abilities, personality, and all the features that make us unique—a masterpiece.

Sometimes, we need to protect what God created with boundaries. A boundary is a predetermined point at which hostile, aggressive, or unwelcome behavior is deemed unacceptable. Boundaries provide us with a stopping point while working through negative behaviors, or as long-term components when dealing with someone, we must maintain a connection.

In any instance, if we feel ongoing disrespect or aggressive behavior threatens our well-being, we can employ a four-step method to limit a person's negative behavior. Here's how boundaries work:

- First, inform the person that we'll not tolerate disrespectful behavior.

- Second, define the boundary and clarify what negative behavior we consider disrespectful.

- Third, inform the person that we'll discontinue interactions once the behavior disrespects the boundary—the consequence.

- Fourth, follow through on the consequences of violating the boundary.

For example, if we say, "If you roll your eyes at me again while we're talking, I will leave the conversation for an hour!" If they persist, stop the conversation for an hour. Never let our warning be an empty threat. If we fail to enforce the boundaries, the person disrespecting us will conclude that our threats have no consequence, and their behavior will continue.

Our best line of defense against dishonorable behavior is establishing and enforcing limitations. We not only gain respect for ourselves, but the other person realizes that we'll not tolerate unacceptable conduct.

While we have no control over how others react to us, we do have power over what we allow into our lives that impacts our well-being. Boundaries, in time, can be removed as the disrespectful tendencies are managed.

Final Thoughts:

When we disrespect each other, we take steps backward and become counterproductive to establishing the relationship we profess we seek.

> *And knowing their thoughts, Jesus said to them, "Every kingdom divided against itself is laid waste; and no city or house divided against itself will stand. (Matthew 12:25)*

If our spouse has betrayed or shown disrespect to us, it can be difficult, or seem impossible, to forgive. If you're at this point in your relationship, you must make a choice. Do I let bitterness continue to govern my emotions and destroy my relationship, or do I learn to forgive and move forward in life?

To overcome conflicts in relationships, we must prioritize love, patience, and a sincere desire to change disrespectful behavior. Remember, If we want to repair what is broken, we can't keep the relationship in a state of brokenness. It's through honor that we find reward.

> *Above all, keep fervent in your love for one another, because love covers a multitude of sins. (1 Peter 4:8)*

Strategy for Success:

- Have those difficult conversations about any disrespectful behaviors causing relationship problems.

- Change anything about our lives that may tempt us to engage in sexual immorality.

- Start removing any temptations in our lives that may lead to disrespectful behavior.

- Never stop dating your spouse.

- Talk with anyone who has been a victim of our dishonoring behavior. Ask for their forgiveness.

- Learn to respect yourself. When needed, set and enforce boundaries for inappropriate behavior.

Related Scripture:

- *Romans 12:9–13*

- *Deuteronomy 5:16*

- *1 Timothy 5:17–18*

- *Hebrews 13:4*

- *Hebrews 13:18*

Let God Fight the Battle:

Holy God,
Please reveal to us how we've disrespected You by disrespecting others.
We seek forgiveness and mercy for our misguided behavior, which may have caused suffering in the hearts of others.
Lord, cleanse our souls of any shame we've brought upon

You, ourselves, or others.
Father, we ask that You replace any hurt we've caused others with peace and comfort found in Your endless love.
May we learn to always honor You with our thoughts, words, and actions as we go forward in life.
I pray these things in the name of our Lord Jesus, Amen.

Chapter Seven
EYE FOR AN I

"Selfishness consumes everything around us until nothing remains, including ourselves."

Growing up, I always counted down to the start of our long-awaited summer break from school. I cherished those days without any thoughts of the classroom and the smell of freshly cooked bacon luring me out of bed. After breakfast, I ventured off on the day's spontaneous adventures, only to be brought back to reality by nighttime curfew.

I cherished those carefree days of my youth until I began working in the watermelon and tobacco fields during the scorching Florida summers to pay for a car. But, before the realities and obligations of adulthood arrived, life was good for that brief period in my childhood.

Looking back, I'm grateful my parents encouraged me to work for what I wanted and needed. Those early teachings in accountability prepared me to be the responsible adult that God expects and society deserves.

> *When I was a child, I used to speak like a child, think like a child, reason like a child; when I became a man, I did away with childish things. (1 Corinthians 13:11)*

Unfortunately, today's culture is slowly breaking away from the foundational values that formerly produced resilient adults who work together to achieve a common goal. "How can I help?" is being replaced by "What's in it for me?" Inevitably, our relationships have also become victims of this all-about-me attitude that promotes self-entitlement.

Some time ago, I had dinner with a young couple who validated our culture's transformation. After a speaking commitment, the seemingly charming duo invited me to dinner—starving, I gladly accepted. The wife considerately suggested that I choose the restaurant. Not knowing the area, I replied that I was okay with whatever they suggested.

She thought for a moment before recommending a place with something on the menu for almost everyone. As she's speaking, the husband interrupts, stating an intense dislike for her proposal and asserting a desire to dine at his favorite nearby restaurant. I'm not a picky eater, so I was fine with whatever they chose. However, I couldn't help but feel bad for the wife, who was interrupted and had her feelings discounted by her husband.

When we arrived at the restaurant, there was a long wait for us to be seated. As we started making small talk to fill the moments, out of nowhere, "This line needs to hurry up. "I've got things to do," interrupted the flow of our social chatting. I began to think that I was the one infringing on his time.

We finally sat, and the husband seldom raised his head during the meal, making him the winner of his secret race to finish first. Impatience oozed from his long face as he waited for us to finish eating. As soon as we set down our utensils, he asked, "Are you two ready? I don't want to miss the game. I might make the kickoff if we hurry."

"I thought we were going to stop by the hobby shop on the way home?" she asked hopefully. Once again, he expressed his desire not to miss the game. There was only the sound of a slow, disappointed sigh being exhaled, knowing her husband had made himself the focus of the entire evening. I could tell she had come to tolerate his self-centered behavior to avoid an argument.

In a relationship, we should help attain and share our wants, needs, and goals as a couple—as a team. When we only think about ourselves, we develop a "single-minded" personality rather than a "couple mentality." We must constantly guard ourselves against the selfish inclinations that can seep in and become routine, impacting our relationships.

When we show love, kindness, and consideration, we receive it when we need it from others. If not, God will balance the scales as our reward.

> *Give, and it will be given to you. They will pour into your lap a good measure—pressed down, shaken together, and*

> *running over. For by your standard of measure it will be measured to you in return. (Luke 6:38)*

From God's Perspective:

Love is not—*self-seeking*

> *do not merely look out for your own personal interests, but also for the interests of others. (Philippians 2:4)*

From Vice to Virtue:

Sitting on the porch, engrossed in the sound of heaven's water gently finding its way to the roof, my cell phone rings, breaking my solitary meditation. It was my best friend from childhood. We hadn't spoken in a while, so we eagerly reminisced and caught up on life—including the news of his marriage engagement.

Growing up, I never imagined him as the marrying type, but the excitement that radiated in his voice revealed his complete surrender to his desire to marry. He went on to inform me about the wedding date and the chosen best man, his brother-in-law. As much as I tried, I could no longer focus on our conversation—I was hurt. I had always assumed that I would be his best man.

In my frustration, I made up a lame last-minute excuse not to attend the wedding. Looking back, I had selfishly made the wedding about myself. My disapproval of his decision triggered jealousy, which impacted both of us—through the years, we lost touch, and we haven't talked since. A lifelong friendship ended because I allowed a jealous moment to ignite my emotions—a modern-day Cain and Abel scenario retold.

I should've kept my emotions in check and supported his special day, not adding resentment by feeling "entitled"—a costly lesson in life with lasting repercussions. I hope my stories about the self-centered husband, making the night about himself, and my retaliating out of egotistical entitlement have illustrated our emotions' negative impact on others.

If we're prone to allowing our personality to be dominated by a self-centered mindset, we must learn to overcome this compromising mentality. Everyone will appreciate the effort we put into making the change into a new, caring, and thoughtful person.

There are a few unmistakable indicators that someone feels entitled, resulting in a selfish disposition. Some are like neon signs, while others are as subtle as a poison ivy outbreak—suddenly, we must deal with the irritating problem.

For awareness, let's examine four of the most typical selfish personality mindsets:

- Others should help me.

- What will I gain from helping?

- I don't have time for this.

- What I'm doing is more important.

Others Should Help Me:

Not receiving help from a stranger may temporarily impact our emotions, but a lack of support from a partner can build animosity and resentment in a relationship. If we believe our partner is self-serving and not a team player—we must gather our thoughts, take a deep breath, and tell them. A discovery talk can help partners identify areas where they have unintentionally failed to support or recognize the other's needs. It will bring clarity.

As with all discovery conversations, our goal is not to establish blame—doing so only causes the person to become defensive. The most fruitful conversations will always be those in which both parties stay open-minded while seeking a mutual solution.

We begin the discussion by expressing our appreciation for what they do—as we've mentioned before, a sweetener for a bitter situation. If we can't think of anything to compliment them on, we may need to honestly look within to determine if we're the source of the problem. Is it conceivable that we've overlooked what they already do and are focused on doing more?

For example, we might agree that cutting the grass is a household necessity that must be addressed. And, while this is true, is it a joint effort or a task that we expect the other spouse to undertake automatically? Another thing to consider—if our partner handles certain obligations for our team, can we expect them to partake equally in the rest of the household chores? We could say, "I'll cut the grass if they will help with the other chores." We could argue that point, but in all fairness, does that statement appreciate and recognize their role in always cutting the grass?

If we search our hearts and discover we've taken for granted an undertaking that our spouse has taken on for our team, in all gratefulness, thank them. Next, extend our consideration by asking if they believe we're equally supporting the shared responsibilities. By not assigning blame and allowing others to express their feelings and needs, we can learn what's needed to establish mutual teamwork in the future. The most important thing to remember is to always express gratitude and not allow one spouse to take on too much of the shared responsibilities.

One thing I've learned about managing people is to provide them with duties they enjoy doing. By doing so, they'll give their all, optimize the process, and feel content while they work, freeing up time for other things. Try discussing the shared duties with your partner and consider whether a change in routine may result in an improved team spirit.

Here's how the dynamics of teamwork should work within the relationship. If we're not helping—contribute in some way beneficial to the common goal. If we're helping, practice complimenting each other for their contribution as long as a common goal remains. Always be mindful of our pronoun usage when stating what we do or don't do as a team. If our spouse is helping, never say "I" am doing or have done this. Say "We."

For instance, suppose a couple wants to paint their home. Unfortunately, only one partner has the skills to paint. They decide that the one who can paint will focus on painting the house while the other focuses on the shared daily tasks. The question is, who is painting the house?

We may argue it's obvious—the individual doing the painting. But dig deep here—while this is a true statement, how about the partner who did all the shared chores while the house was being painted? Did they contribute to the cause, the common goal? Our perception of how the house was painted may reveal much about our sense of teamwork.

Let's take an example from the dynamics of a football team. Every team needs a skilled quarterback who can deliver the ball accurately to the intended player. Although without the massive lineman protecting the quarterback, giving him time to throw the ball, the team would not advance down the field to score a touchdown. In reality, they need each other to score the win.

Teams are made up of other people who contribute their unique skills to achieve a common objective. So, let's revisit our previous questions. Who painted the couple's house? Is cutting the grass not to be considered help? How do we perceive our partner? Is it their selfishness to help more or our neglect to recognize what they already do to support the team?

Remember, we are seeking a culture of working as a team, not performing a single job. A culture will only emerge if we maintain a mutual balance of obligations, a show of gratitude, and an ongoing supportive, collaborative process. Always appreciate each other—as a loving and grateful team. When people feel valued, they're more likely to support positive changes. Help others break the self-centered cycle by setting an example.

> *Why do you look at the speck*
> *that is in your brother's eye,*
> *but do not notice the log that*

> *is in your own eye? Or how can you say to your brother, 'Let me take the speck out of your eye,' and look, the log is in your own eye? You hypocrite, first take the log out of your own eye, and then you will see clearly to take the speck out of your brother's eye!* (Matthew 7:3–5)

What Will I Gain from Helping?

A childhood friend once stated, "I'll help you if you help me." It was the first encounter I can recall with a verbal contract consisting of exchanging promises to repay a service. I'm sure we've all experienced this innocent form of bartering that teaches us to rely on one another to achieve objectives. As we mature, this early learned fundamental re-payment system becomes unnecessary—for most of us.

Unfortunately, a selfish person often continues expecting re-payment for services rendered—unless they're the person needing help. A self-centered individual will seldom aid someone if there's nothing to gain. So, how do we deal with those who expect something in return for their help? We could inform them that if they don't help us, we won't help when they need something. While this strategy is inviting, it requires us to regress and use childish methods to solve an adult problem.

The best approach is to engage in a discovery conversation to understand why they need compensation for their support. Perhaps they believe we're not doing enough to help them. In fairness, we should check ourselves with an open mind to ensure we're supporting them as needed. Sometimes, we can get busy with life and overlook our spouse's need for help—it happens.

The problem could also be from unresolved emotions from previous "single-minded" relationships, family, friends, or coworkers. If so, approach the situation with compassion and patience. Reassure them that our goal is to establish a team of mutual support in times of need—without compensation. We must keep in mind that change takes time. It took time for the problem to surface, and it will take time to resolve with love, patience, and consistency, with no expectations from the person.

Why no expectations? We must never impose an underlying price on kindness, which we seek to change in our partners—lead by example.

> *But love your enemies, and do good, and lend, expecting nothing in return; and your reward will be great, and you will be sons of the Most High; for He Himself is kind to ungrateful and evil men. (Luke 6:35)*

I Don't Have Time for This:

When we first started dating our spouse, we wished we could slow time, prolonging every euphoric moment. We likely spent countless hours with our phones plastered to our ears and finding any excuse to send a quick text throughout the day. Suddenly, it appeared that our need to maintain our smitten trends began fading. What changed?

If we don't keep the romance kindled, the daily routine of life will slowly suffocate the relationship. Our connection with our partners is alive and must breathe; it needs our attention to thrive and blossom into the healthy, loving relationships we desire. Daily responsibilities, family, friends, career, and personal goals consume much of our time and can upset the balance of life and relationships. While all of these responsibilities are important, time with our partners should always be a priority. Marriage counselors recommend prioritizing a weekly date night.

Date night can be a great way to stay connected. Note—avoid engaging in activities where you won't be interacting with each other. A word on cell phones—your date won't feel their importance if you can't control the urge to browse social media, text, or answer a call that can wait. Look around in the public places you visit, and you'll see couples sitting beside each other on their phone. It pains my heart to see so many couples squandering precious bonding time and then asking what's wrong with their relationships. No excuses—stop letting your phone have more attention than your date.

Time together should be spent discovering each other and having fun—feeding the relationship. If we don't know our spouse's interests, we ask questions. Hint—if we've no idea what our partner likes, it's a sign that we're not prioritizing the relationship. Quality time spent getting to know each other strengthens the relational bond and prepares us for life together. It helps to build our team that not only shares the obligations in life but also the joyous times. So, how can we balance everything life throws and devote quality time to our relationships? The key is balance and priority.

Years ago, my father explained how a 60/40 time management rule helps maintain a balance in life. Our jobs, family, friends, maintenance, projects, and goals comprise sixty percent of our time. The remaining forty percent should always be set aside for our commitment to our spouse—without excuses.

I've heard it said that marriage is a 50/50 proposition—that's not a possible reality. It's neither realistic nor conceivable to always provide equal support to one another. There will be times when life demands more of us than we can give, and this is when we must rely on our partner, our teammate.

When our spouse is overwhelmed by life, we must be supportive. It may disrupt our plans temporarily, but by helping during difficult times, we feed our relationship and starve any selfish impulses that may exist in our personality. Once our partner has helped us overcome our time of need, we in turn, help them catch up on the things they may have neglected while showing us support.

Always prioritize the things that matter most—our relationships and spending time in prayer to become the unselfish partner God intended.

What I'm Doing Is More Important:

Have you ever awoken knowing the day would be an epic disaster? I'm sure most of us can relate to the scenario below...

I've hit the snooze button too many times, ignoring the relentless reminder of a fresh day—now I'm late for work. I frantically dress like an unsupervised toddler, dashing out of the house and into the car, hoping to arrive at work on time.

To make matters worse, I missed the green light at a four-way traffic light. My wife has sent a text message, and I'm trying to reply when a loud beeping interrupts my focus. I look up and see that the light is green. The annoying sound of the horn continues.

Frustrated, I hurried through the traffic light and almost collided with a car in front of me—a cop. As I passed, hoping the officer hadn't noticed, I saw their lights flashing in my rearview mirror and heard the sound of the siren motioning me to pull over. The officer steps out of their cruiser, advances toward me, and stands at my car window, his face emotionless and formal.

I apologetically inform the officer, "I shouldn't have been driving so carelessly. I'm running late for work, so I was trying to make up some time. I'm so sorry. "

The officer responds with revelation, "Did you consider that you might have contributed to those behind you being late for work also?" I suddenly realized what a jerk I'd been. I had selfishly imposed on everyone else's day by trying to fulfill my needs. All because I felt my situation and what I was doing took precedence over others.

The fictitious scenario above depicts how our actions can impact those around us—the scientific law of cause and effect.

Everyone's time is invaluable, and we should never prioritize our objectives over those of others. That way of thinking encourages selfishness, which hinders our success in life and relationships.

When we feel anxiety growing in our minds, Shelah and I will both convey how we're feeling and rely on one another for a voice of encouragement. This approach of soothing our stressful situations is part of being a team and the cornerstone of the previously described 60/40 rule of support.

There's power in the words of a loved one.

> *Anxiety in a person's heart weighs it down, But a good word makes it glad. (Proverbs 12:25)*

Final Thoughts:

Kindness is the virtue that will triumph against selfishness. At times, it might seem that we'll not attain our goals if we stop and help our partners. With a team approach, both partners can balance time and effort by easing burdens and navigating the challenges of life in collaboration.

The team mindset involves both partners having an ongoing consideration for what the other has going on in life. I want us to take a moment and consider how we "thank" our partners. Do we say "thank you" and go about our business, leaving them to finish what they were doing before helping us? If so, isn't that a conditioned response to express thanks rather than one that fosters a cultured atmosphere for relational support?

When our spouse offers their time to help us, turn and ask if there's anything we can do to help them in return. When asked if we need help, don't try to be the hero by saying no—that won't help establish teamwork in a relationship. Accept their offer, enjoy the time spent together, and smile, knowing you're cultivating the team mentality needed for lasting relationships. A win-win situation for both partners.

We've now removed "single-mindedness" and replaced it with a "couple" mentality. Not only have we begun to form a team environment, but we've also helped remove the obstacle that impedes us as individuals—selfishness.

Working as a team brings priceless memories that bind us as a couple. From these moments of unity, we draw security and faith in facing the challenges ahead. When we fail to support one another as a team, the spouse who believes the scales are imbalanced will become resentful of the unfair situation.

We must never lose sight of our relationship as the highest priority, second only to God. We can't honestly say we prioritize our relationship if we spend most of our time elsewhere. If we choose not to prioritize the relationship, we fail to take the wisdom of God seriously—a recipe for disaster.

Strategy for Success:

- Practice putting others ahead of ourselves. Begin by letting someone go ahead of us in a long line—small things develop into big things.

- Replace the "single-minded" mentality with "couple-minded" thinking.

- Look for ways to foster a "team" mentality.

- Work toward creating a culture and being supportive that will sustain the nature of working together at all times and all obstacles.

- Make time to support each other using the 60/40 rule.

- Break free from past experiences that encourage selfish behavior. If needed, talk to your partner and for support as we work through them.

Related Scripture:

- *Philippians 2:4*

- *1 John 3:17*

- *1 Corinthians 10:24*

- *Galatians 6:2*

- *Romans 15:1–3*

Let God Fight the Battle:

> *Father God,*
> *Help us to always seek to put You above all else in our lives.*
> *We ask for a humble and generous heart that will overcome our selfish tendencies.*
> *Help us to remember that all our needs and blessings are met through You alone.*
> *In the precious name of Jesus, we ask all things,*
> *Amen.*

Chapter Eight
Mad About You

"Managed anger fades like the sunset, but when uncontrolled and released, it can create those lasting memories we wish we could delete."

To save money, I had chosen to dig an underground utility trench for a country homesite I was developing. It was a hot summer day, forcing the leaves on the trees to fold into themselves to hide from the sun. At this point, the sweltering heat had me second-guessing my hasty decision in an attempt to save money. Nonetheless, defiantly, I proceeded to the proposed trench location.

As I began digging, I noticed the ground was mostly sand, making retrieving shovels full of dirt challenging. After a while of digging, huge mounds formed on the side of the trench, making it difficult to stack the next shovel of dirt. To make matters worse, half of the excavated sand kept falling back into the trench, collapsing the walls and increasing my workload—and frustration.

I can feel my emotions escalating out of control as salty sweat drips down my forehead and into my eyes, blurring my vision. In a fit of rage, I sprang out of the trench, breaking the shovel over my knee and declaring, "I'm finished. "I don't care if the trench is ever dug." Defeated, I proceeded to take refuge from the blistering sun underneath a nearby live oak tree, whose massive ancient limbs seemed to wrap around me in a motherly way, calming me down.

I sat for a time, appreciating the gentle breeze that had joined forces with the shaded tree canopy to help ease my troubled situation. Feeling revitalized, I prepared to finish what I started and go another round with that trench of suffering.

Before confronting my adversary, I would have to purchase a new shovel. On the way to the hardware store, I reflected on how my emotions had gotten the best of me, causing me to lose control. I could have avoided my frustrations by:

- Not rushing into a potentially stressful situation to save a few dollars.

- Willing to pay someone to dig the trench with machinery.

- Not working in the blistering heat of the midday sun.

- Moistening the earth to prevent it from falling back into the trench.

- Purchasing a trench shovel designed for the task.

- Purchasing gloves to prevent the numerous painful

blisters that had formed on my hands.

Summing up, I could've done numerous things to prevent "triggering" my anger. A trigger is a person, place, or thing that can interrupt a calm mental state and cause us to overreact. It could be bumping into someone from a previous relationship, being caught in traffic, or having a horrible trench-digging experience.

We're human—everyone has potential triggers, and we must accept responsibility when they occur and begin to implement strategies to help us avoid them in the future. Our outburst of emotions that damage our relationships is our responsibility, and we must stop blaming circumstances—or others.

> *for the anger of man does not produce the righteousness of God. (James 1:20)*

From God's Perspective:

Love is not—*easily angered*

> *Let all bitterness and wrath and anger and clamor and slander be put away from you, along with all malice. Be kind to one another, tender-hearted, forgiving each*

> *other, just as God in Christ also has forgiven you. (Ephesians 4:31–32)*

From Vice to Virtue:

It may seem that taking personal accountability will only cause additional issues in the relationship. It does momentarily, but it serves an essential long-term purpose. Without accountability, unresolved issues that cause problems will continue to cause friction in our relationships. By accepting accountability, we can begin to identify and reduce the elements that can interrupt our happy, controlled mental state—those pesky triggers.

Let's go over some of the most prevalent catalysts with the potential to cause distress and may deserve our attention:

- Impatience
- Defensiveness
- Retaliation
- Denial
- Paranoid
- Addiction

Impatience:

Christmas was always my most anticipated holiday as a child. Its arrival marked a nice change from the steamy Florida summers to more comfortable winter weather. It also meant the possibility of scoring the gifts I'd hinted at all year.

As an adult, I still love the holidays but have come to dread assembling purchased items with several bags of parts and pages of small font instructions. To avoid this, I try not to buy gifts requiring assembly and recognize that if necessary, the assembly fee imposed by stores is money well spent.

Instructions may be unclear, something may not fit, parts may be missing, or we're pressed for time—numerous possibilities can trigger negative emotions. Similarly, when we're unable to resolve a relational issue, we can become upset, and our aggravation and anxiety can swiftly escalate into anger.

Allowing time to calm down and rethink the situation is always the best approach to dealing with frustration. For success, we must remain composed and follow one resolution step at a time, in order, much like reading instructions—we can't rush the process.

I've learned that the following steps are essential for successfully addressing relationship issues:

1. Patience

2. Discovery

3. Accountability

4. Forgiveness

5. Resolution

If we skip a step, we may never reach the resolution stage of the process. We can't resolve an unknown problem—we must discover it. We can't begin forgiveness until we know what to forgive—take accountability. It's only logical that if we skip steps, the process could fail, and we may lose hope of overcoming the problem.

Once we lose hope, it can lead to anxiety, leading to more frustration. We must remember that the success of our marriage is God's will. Our responsibility is to remain patient and remain faithful that God will provide the remedy to our circumstances.

> *And which of you by worrying can add a single hour to his lifespan? If then you cannot do even a very little thing, why do you worry about other matters? (Luke 12:25–26)*

Defensiveness:

Defense is a natural, God-given element of our humanity necessary for survival. That same protective instinct is often used to avoid dealing with relational issues—defensiveness leading to deflection. If we want to overcome unwelcome relational conduct, we must not tolerate or craft any diversionary methods meant to obstruct the resolution process.

If our partner uses becomes defensive to avoid communication, respectfully let them know you'd like to continue later. By taking this approach, you respect and accept their desire not to continue the conversation momentarily but haven't dismissed the problem. Our goal is to allow time for them to calm down, understand the need for an open discovery conversation, and begin the resolution process without using any of the blocking methods.

If they continue to use the defensive approach, pose the question only they can answer: "Something is negatively impacting the relationship—what's wrong?" Direct communication stresses the need for an answer that will help in defining the problem. This strategy helps to eliminate the potential of denial and for them to ignore the issue.

One thing to remember about all problems, there's no such thing as made up or nonexistent. We may not know the root cause at first, and it may not be what is on display, but something is causing havoc in the relationship—that's not made up. This is why I constantly refer to "discovery" conversations: to find the trigger's foundational cause and become proactive in its resolution.

> *The way of a fool is right in his own eyes, but a person who listens to advice is wise.*
> *(Proverbs 12:15)*

Retaliation:

When a partner doesn't accept the outcome of a situation, they may isolate themselves from the usual routine of the relationship—they retaliate. This could entail retreating from spending time together, refraining from the typical love expressions, name-calling, insinuations, breaking things, or even sharing secrets. I'm sure we've all resorted to some form of retaliation at some point.

The trouble with erecting walls or getting even is that it doesn't solve anything and only worsens matters. I remember a coworker telling me a heartbreaking story about her cheating spouse—she was devastated, to say the least. While shopping, one of her close girlfriends spotted her husband having lunch with an attractive woman and relayed the observations to protect her friend. In her grief and to retaliate, she arranged to have lunch with an admirer the following weekend who had been making attempts toward her.

After her revenge date, she later discovered the lady witnessed with her husband had hired him to do handyman jobs for extra money—to help buy her a nice birthday gift. She was simply repaying him for his hard work by buying him lunch. Lesson—things aren't always what they seem, and we should never assume. Can you imagine how she must have felt discovering the truth after succumbing to her spiteful retaliation date? Can you imagine what her husband felt? We must remember that a vengeful deed committed today may be a regretful memory tomorrow.

Retaliation is an unfounded act of revenge, only serving to cause a greater division within the partnership. Consider this: would we rather work on the problem causing us emotional distress or add another one to the list, inflicting further damage to the relationship?

> *Never pay back evil with more evil. Do things in such a way that everyone can see you are honorable. (Romans 12:17)*

Denial:

Our pride can make it difficult to admit fault or reveal our flaws—pride must be conquered. For a successful relationship, we need accountability with ourselves and each other, and pride hinders this process.

During a rough period in my life, I turned to alcohol. My evening ritual drink became the perfect escape to avoid dealing with the overwhelming negative situations that surrounded me—my excuse. I was living in denial, believing that I harmlessly drank to unwind. The truth is that drinking had become a vice disguised as solace that I had refused to recognize as a problem—the foundation for denial. Only when I began following Jesus did I truly understand He's all we need. Through Him, I started recognizing and accepting accountability and was able to begin eradicating problems from my life.

Denial of a problem will continue to slowly chip away at the relationship's well-being. Don't spend years wasting precious time when freedom is in sight. Search your heart—if change is needed, have those hard talks with your partner. I'm sure they already know and have been waiting for you to acknowledge the issues causing distance in the relationship. Use the discovery process to isolate the issue and work through the problem if needed. Remember, patience with a dash of love is the key to overcoming the hard struggles we face.

> *Better to be patient than powerful; better to have self-control than to conquer a city. (Proverbs 16:32)*

Paranoid:

Anger is typically the result of unresolved issues or triggers that cause us to lose control of our emotions. This constant battle with frustration can lead to paranoid tendencies. Paranoia can sometimes make us feel as if people are trying to get us, raising our levels of frustration and causing us to sleep poorly. Once this happens, a person may feel trapped in this reactionary state of releasing frustration, followed by remorse, leading to paranoia—a vicious cycle.

Getting proper rest is the best method to reduce our frustration levels, improve problem-solving abilities, reduce paranoia, increase stamina, and avoid many serious medical conditions. If we're suffering from sleep deprivation or a more serious underlying emotional condition, we should schedule an appointment with medical professionals.

> *For God has not given us a spirit of fear, but of power and of love and of a sound mind. (2 Timothy 1:7)*

Addiction:

Addiction causes anger and has affected many marriages, but it can be overcome through unyielding prayer, patience, persistence, and professional counseling. Schedule the needed appointments that will offer hope and help to safeguard our relationships.

> *Who has woe? Who has sorrow? Who has contentions? Who has complaining? Who has wounds without cause? Who has redness of eyes? Those who linger long over wine, Those who go to taste mixed wine. Do not look on the wine when it is red, When it sparkles in the cup, When it goes down smoothly; At the last it bites like a serpent and stings like a viper. Your eyes will see strange*

> *things and your mind will utter perverse things. And you will be like the one who lies down in the middle of the sea, Or like one who lies down on the top of a mast. They struck me, but I did not become ill; They beat me, but I did not know it. When shall I awake? I will seek another drink. (Proverbs 23:29-35)*

Working Through the Anger:

Anger issues rarely fix themselves, demanding uncomfortable conversations to resolve. The timing of the discussion is a crucial factor to avoid further compounding the situation. Never try to express emotional feelings when one or both parties are hungry, irritated, or pressed for time.

Wait until you're both relaxed and capable of being good listeners before proceeding, remembering to address one topic at a time. Never wildly express frustrations that lead away from the main topic—it will only prolong the process and lead to more anxiety in the relationship.

Begin with something like, "I'd like to discuss why you seem unhappy. Is it okay if we talk?" This tone is not threatening, demanding, or judgmental. Listen intently, allowing them to express their feelings—validation. We cannot tell someone how to feel, but we can listen respectfully and understand that it's a real concern for them.

If we're the victim of an abusive relationship, we may naturally be tempted to lash out during conversations—control this urge. Uncontrolled outbursts of criticism may incite unwanted hostility or prematurely end discussions. The goal is to achieve unity by discovering and resolving issues with patience, understanding, determination, and kindness—not assigning blame or condemnation. We must keep the resolution process alive.

Severe or in-depth issues may require additional discussions, therapy, and repeated attempts before finding a resolution. The worst mistake is to be impatient and keep pushing for a solution. We must remember to take breaks and allow the problem to breathe.

Have you ever noticed how less distracted we feel after a vacation? A more complex issue may benefit from a couple's vacation and temporarily forgetting about the situation. Humans are like mechanical toys—we don't perform well when the batteries run low. We all need the occasional break to recharge.

Following a period of revitalization, we should return our focus on incorporating strategies for stress reduction into our routines. Make a list of "stressors" that can be eliminated or managed while maintaining supportive communication. Remember, one of the best proactive conversations that support and dispel anger begins with, "I understand how you feel."

> *with all humility and gentleness, with patience, showing tolerance for one another*

> *in love, being diligent to preserve the unity of the Spirit in the bond of peace. (Ephesians 4:2–3)*

The most essential thing to remember while dealing with conflicts is not to allow them to grow into something bigger. When we have an unresolved problem in our relationship, we're naturally less responsive or tend to avoid spending time together—avoid this trap. Spend as much quality time together as possible while working through the obstacles.

Resolving the sometimes hidden or deep-rooted relational issues can take time—be patient. To soothe my overpowering frustrations with a situation, I often reflect on *The Serenity Prayer*, which has often helped me put life into perspective. In logical simplicity, it asserts that life is a choice between being content and letting our emotions dominate us.

> *God, give us the grace to accept with serenity the things that cannot be changed, the courage to change the things which should be changed, and the wisdom to distinguish the one from the other. Living one day at a time, enjoying one moment at a time, accepting hardship as a pathway to peace, taking, as Jesus did, this sinful world as it is, not as I would have it, trusting that You will make all things right, if I surrender to Your will, so that I may be reasonably happy in this life, and supremely happy with You forever in the next. Amen.* -Reinhold Niebuhr

Final Thoughts:

The everyday challenges we face can often overwhelm us and cause us to lash out at others unintentionally. Life will continue to throw obstacles our way, so we must learn to manage how we respond by accepting what we can and cannot control.

Imagine an angry lion with a thorn lodged in its paw. Everything will irritate the beast until the perpetrator, the thorn, is removed. Sometimes, we become the lion with a thorn in our paw—adversity accumulates and drives us to lash out at others.

Being a problem solver who can manage negative emotions during trying times is indispensable for the success of our relationship. If we fail to put in the effort to have the difficult conversations without any strategies to block the problem, our anger will continue to destroy the relationship we cherish.

When problems emerge, and they will, we must remember to focus on resolving the temporary obstacle rather than venting anger on our permanent loved ones. If allowed, anger will eat away at the joy in our relationships, tarnishing everything beautiful that was, is, or might have been.

Strategy for Success:

- Follow the steps for resolving an anger problem: Discovery, Acceptance, Accountability, asking for Forgiveness, and Resolution.

- Have the difficult conversations about our anger

problems. Wait for the right time when not overcome with frustration or anger.

- Identify "triggers" and "stressors"—avoid them.

- Address one problem at a time. Overwhelming ourselves can lead to frustration.

- Learn to control the desire to become defensive, retaliatory, or critical during interactions.

- Seek counseling for deep-rooted issues, paranoia, or substance abuse.

- Practice *The Serenity Prayer* in our daily thinking.

Related Scripture:

- *Psalm 37:8*
- *Proverbs 14:29*
- *Ephesians 4:26*
- *James 1:19–20*
- *Proverbs 29:11*

Let God Fight the Battle:

Heavenly Father,
Help us to resist any emotions that may dishonor You or others.
Lord, reveal to us any matters witin our hearts that may cause uncontrolled anger.
Guide us in overcoming any past issues causing us to fall short of Your goodness.
May Your perfect mercy forever embrace our relationships with grace.
In the name of our Lord Jesus, we ask these things,
Amen.

Chapter Nine
Two Wrongs Too Long

"We sometimes impose self-inflicted imprisonment because of our differences or mistakes, knowing that the path to liberation is within our hearts."

Do you ever reminisce about how perfect and refreshing life seemed when you first met your spouse? Life was perfect in every way, leaving us counting the minutes until we could once again spend time with the flawless object of our adoration. While caught up in this blissful state of mind, we somehow missed little blemishes in their personality that would ordinarily upset us.

Slowly, the relationship settles into a routine, and the ignored trivial quirks become irritations. We begin to reflect on what happened, hoping for a solution to restore the relationship to its former splendor. The truth—the excitement of the new relationship temporarily obscured noticing each other's flaws. As I've heard it said, "The honeymoon is over."

This sudden shift may take us by surprise if we're reluctant to acknowledge the imperfections of our humanity and the differences in our individuality. Everyone has an acceptance threshold for others and what we consider normal conduct. When these contrasts are exceeded, they can alter our emotions and define how forgiving we are of diversified personalities.

My father was the most composed, understanding, and forgiving man I've known. He always welcomed people as they were and never attempted to mold them into what he thought they should be. When I made a mistake, he accepted it and always granted forgiveness, knowing that I would make more. Most importantly, we always started over the next day. I would later hear that same comforting assurance from another source I've come to cherish.

> *The LORD'S loving kindnesses indeed never cease, For His compassions never fail. They are new every morning; Great is Your faithfulness. (Lamentations 3:22–23)*

God's never-ending mercy allows us to start each day fresh, indicating our need for constant forgiveness. Just as God graciously reconciles with us when we make mistakes, we must also allow others to obtain our forgiveness.

> *If we say that we have no sin, we are deceiving ourselves and the truth is not in us. If we confess our sins, He is faithful and righteous to forgive us our sins and to cleanse us from all unrighteousness. If we say that we have not sinned, we make Him a liar and His word is not in us. (1 John 1:8–10)*

From God's Perspective:

Love does not—*keeps no record of wrongs*

> *Let all bitterness and wrath and anger and clamor and slander be put away from you, along with all malice. Be kind to one another, tender-hearted, forgiving each other, just as God in Christ also has forgiven you. (Ephesians 4:31–32)*

From Vice to Virtue:

When I have habitual sin in my life that I'm trying to remove, no matter how hard I try, I don't feel very spiritual. I seem to nervously pray as if I'm speaking to a parent who is aware of the unacceptable behavior that I'm trying to conceal. Scripture isn't read and studied with the same enthusiasm and passion, resulting in a weakened spiritual connection with God. As time goes by, guilt accumulates even more, distancing the division further.

We feel the same separation in our relationships when we refuse to forgive our partner for their mistakes. If someone has wronged us, we must either work it out with them or let it go by surrendering it to God. Relationships cannot thrive in a resentful environment and may eventually implode.

Consider this: If we've just fought, would we turn to our spouse and ask them to go on a fun date in the hopes of an intimate evening? It probably wouldn't turn out so well—we must first fix the underlying problem.

When conflict disrupts the rhythm of the relationship, the perpetrator must recognize, admit responsibility, and seek forgiveness. Likewise, the victim must be willing to forgive the incident—it takes two willing partners to get past conflict. If we can't remember or figure out what's creating the separation, God will show us if we ask.

> *Search me, O God, and know my heart; try me and know my anxious thoughts; and see if there be any hurtful way in me, and lead me in*

> *the everlasting way. (Psalm 139:23-24)*

If forgiveness isn't an essential component of the connection, we'll repeatedly experience the unpleasant emotions of the past, impeding relational growth. God also acknowledges the significance of our forgiveness toward one another.

> *For if you forgive others for their transgressions, your heavenly Father will also forgive you. But if you do not forgive others, then your Father will not forgive your transgressions. (Matthew 6:14-15)*

Sometimes, no matter how hard we try, our best efforts to forgive fail or the person we've hurt refuses to accept our sincere apologies. Certain transgressions inflict deep wounds that take time to heal, making forgiveness difficult to achieve—be patient.

When confronted with a hardened heart, remember the Serenity Prayer's lesson: "Some things we cannot change." In faith, we must cast our eyes to heaven in prayer, believing that God wants us to reconcile what's broken.

> *And looking at them Jesus said to them, "With people*

> *this is impossible, but with God all things are possible." (Matthew 19:26)*

I once heard a moving story about a wife who had prayed for eighteen years for her husband's constant abusive behavior to stop. With enthusiasm and unrelenting patience, she tried advice from several secular marriage publications, went to counseling, and prayed daily for a change. Nothing seemed to work, and she had come to terms with the reality that divorce was the only alternative.

Two weeks before filing, he accepted Jesus Christ into his life. A new person emerged because of God's unending compassion and mercy and his wife's unwavering faith in prayer. With renewed hope, she proclaimed her joy of the rekindled marriage from the rooftops. Through forgiveness, they also put the bitterness of the past behind them. Never underestimate the power of patience, forgiveness, and continuous prayer—love never fails.

So, what happens if the person keeps repeating the offense? Jesus speaks to the measure of our need for ongoing forgiveness:

> *Then Peter came and said to Him, "Lord, how often shall my brother sin against me and I forgive him? Up to seven times?" Jesus said to him, "I do not say to you, up to seven times, but up to sev-*

enty times seven. (Matthew 18:21-22)

Why does Jesus say we must keep forgiving others? As flawed individuals, we cannot avoid mistakes or achieve perfect love, resulting in our continual need for forgiveness. We must adopt an apologetic and forgiving mindset to coexist peacefully. Forgiveness will always be the defining measure of whether our relationships are successful.

Does forgiveness stipulate forgetting what happened? Forgiveness isn't about forgetting but rather not allowing an offense to continue regurgitating and governing our emotions and actions. This begs the question of how do we know if we've wholeheartedly forgiven someone. Simple—the offense will no longer trigger our emotions.

So, as those who have been chosen of God, holy and beloved, put on a heart of compassion, kindness, humility, gentleness and patience; bearing with one another, and forgiving each other, whoever has a complaint against anyone; just as the Lord forgave you, so also should you. Beyond all these things put on love, which

> *is the perfect bond of unity.*
> *Colossians 3:12–14)*

We begin the transition that breaks the shackles of deep-rooted resentment by leveraging the essential qualities of a compassionate person. Some of the most apparent indicators of a naturally forgiving personality are:

- Patient listener

- Unyielding faith

- Strengthens others

- Focuses on present and future

- Readily forgives

Patient Listener:

We cannot begin to solve or offer forgiveness for what we don't fully understand—right? Being a good listener bridges the unclarity of the unknown and allows us to work our way through the steps that lead to solutions.

We must learn to listen to understand so we can relate to the other person's feelings. Why? Because it's important to understand what we need to overcome and forgive—the root cause. If we fail to identify what "triggered" the occurrence, it will likely happen again.

The trap we want to avoid when resolving a problem is resisting the urge to say, "I'm sorry," and "It's ok, I accept your apology" without the issue being resolved. While we want the relationship to return to the loving and harmonious connection we had, it will only be a matter of time before the issue arises again, if not truly resolved.

> *A fool does not delight in understanding, But only in revealing his own mind.*
> *(Proverbs 18:2)*

Unyielding Faith:

When I was growing up, one of the unspoken rules in our home was forgiveness. It went without saying that if a problem arose, we'd work until it was fixed, not to be brought up in conversation again to be revisited. As an adult, I lean on that wisdom in my daily life. Probably not as much as I should, but it's a never-ending endeavor.

If we practice ongoing forgiveness, we will strengthen the bond and security of the relationship. When confronted with relational strife, our thoughts, words, and actions (TWA) will adopt a more laid-back approach, knowing that the final objective will be to achieve unity and reconciliation.

If forgiveness isn't the habitual goal, transgressions will accumulate, making forgiveness more challenging to obtain in the future. When we empower forgiveness, unforgiven wrongs can no longer fester, causing enmity and division. We reclaim control of the once-lost connection and transform it into one that we desire, and that will endure.

We also become more accepting of each other's imperfections and individualism, which leads to freedom and can reawaken our sentiments of affection for our partner. A dwindling flame can be rekindled—we only need unyielding faith in each other and God.

> *When we get together, I want to encourage you in your faith, but I also want to be encouraged by yours. (Romans 1:12)*

Strengthens Others:

When we forgive freely, we empower and define the patience, kindness, and compassion within us, setting an example for others. Our consistent and sincere outward expression of compassion may be enough to soften the heart of someone unwilling to forgive someone else. We never know who is looking to us for the best approach or solution to their dilemma in life.

Once we've experienced the power of forgiveness, we can appreciate the tremendous freedom it brings and become more willing to forgive. We also encourage and empower others to forgive the imprisonment of forgiveness and play the golden rule forward.

> *Do to others as you would have them do to you. (Luke 6:31)*

Focuses on Present and Future:

During college, I worked forty hours weekly as an engineering co-op for American Standard while a full-time student. I would study whenever I could while still trying to spend as much time as possible with my family. With barely three hours of sleep per night, the long workdays and study sessions began to take their toll.

One morning before work, with heavy eyes, I began my study routine. I powered on my laptop and made myself a cup of coffee. Reaching across my laptop to get some study materials, I spilled my freshly poured coffee all over the keypad. With a spark, it abruptly shut down—panic ensued.

The laptop held my final exams for three classes, study notes, resources, and the next semester's carefully planned schedule. The tension seemed like a vice around my skull, causing a lot of negativity that I shared with others at work and school. At the end of the day, I was left with the guilt of my unjustifiable attitude toward others, as well as a damaged laptop that my terrible attitude failed to fix.

Lesson learned—crying over "spilled milk" never remedies a problem. The milk won't pick itself up and return to its container. We can only clean up the mess and be more careful in the future. Life is like driving down an unknown highway. We must keep looking forward, not in the rearview mirror, or we'll collide or drive by something beautiful that lies ahead. We must learn to forgive the past we can't change, focus on the present, and think optimistically about the future.

Readily Forgives:

Unfortunately, forgiveness doesn't always arrive as soon as we'd prefer. If the wound is deeply imprinted, a great deal of pain may be associated, preventing the victim from readily forgiving the perpetrator.

If there are multiple issues, each one must be patiently addressed. The same process of discovery, acceptance, and accountability, which leads to forgiveness, should be used for each related offense. Substance abuse is a perfect instance of a problem that will typically include a multitude of deep-rooted issues that must be treated gradually and incrementally.

When dealing with addiction, everyone concerned must recognize the gravity of the situation and remain compassionate toward one another. Remember that everyone affected by addiction is on the same path to recovering their relationships. As progress is made, we must avoid insinuating or minimizing what each person is going through—each has a different battle.

We also need to be aware of potential regression or relapse—remember that praise strengthens, whereas criticism further weakens the spirit. The struggle with addiction is powerful and real, making it challenging to sustain normal behavior—be patient and ready to offer ongoing forgiveness if needed.

> *For what I am doing, I do not understand; for I am not practicing what I would like to do, but I am doing the very thing I hate. (Romans 7:15)*

Addiction causes us to respond in unexpected ways and do things we wouldn't ordinarily do. We win the battle of the will by having faith in God, swallowing our pride, accepting support from family and friends, and seeking professional counseling as necessary. Most importantly, stay in prayer—God can fix what we think is impossible. We will find strength through the power of His love and patience, which allows us to forgive.

> *Jesus looked at them and said, "With man this is impossible, but with God all things are possible." (Matthew 19:26)*

How to Forgive the Deep Hurt:

Sometimes, we may find it hard to forgive someone who has left us with severe emotional scars from acts such as an affair or physical abuse. Understandably, some offenses can prove challenging to dismiss. Is it even possible to forgive such deep hurt? Yes—we can forgive all injustices in time with God's help.

To comprehend our capacity to forgive, we must consider the extent of God's unconditional love and willingness to forgive. As we talked about in a previous chapter, through an unending love for us, God sent His son Jesus to be the sacrifice for our sins. While Jesus was nailed to the cross dying, He asked His Father to forgive His executioners.

> *But Jesus was saying, "Father forgive them; for they know not what they are doing." And they cast lots, dividing up His garments among themselves. (Luke 23:34)*

God understands our need for forgiveness in all aspects of our lives and will guide and comfort us as we forgive what we thought we couldn't. God will not ask us to do something we aren't capable of doing, and He asks that we forgive others so we can be forgiven.

> *For if you forgive other people for their offenses, your heavenly Father will also forgive you. (Matthew 6:14)*

Forgiveness is about removing the mountains that divide us by doing what we need for ourselves, not what others deserve. By forgiving, we can move on with our lives, free of any animosity we may harbor. A relationship should not be a narrative of old grudges but of understanding, love, and tolerance.

> *Love prospers when a fault is forgiven, but dwelling on it separates close friends. (Proverbs 17:9)*

Final Thoughts:

Carrying grudges from the past will simply increase our attachment to the offenses, allowing them to continue to burden us. Interacting will become increasingly difficult over time—before we know it, we've created a mountain of negativity that divides us.

We must remove any prideful holds preventing us from accepting or offering that much-needed, long-awaited forgiveness. Fight for the love you once knew with your spouse and rekindle that flame of passion. Through the freedom of forgiveness, love, and faith, we can move mountains.

> *If I have the gift of prophecy, and know all mysteries and all knowledge; and if I have all faith, so as to remove mountains, but do not have love, I am nothing. (1 Corinthians 13:2)*

Strategy for Success:

- Remember that God forgives us and wants us to forgive each other.

- Acknowledge that everyone makes mistakes and will continue to do so.

- Ask God to reveal any issues we need to reconcile with others.

- Make a list of offenses we own—seek resolution with all parties if possible.

- Be a compassionate and understanding listener.

- Focus on the present and future—let go of the past we've no control over. Stop looking in the rearview mirror of life.

Related Scripture:

- *Ephesians 4:32*
- *Luke 17:3–4*
- *Luke 6:37*
- *Colossians 3:13*

- *Proverbs 10:12*

Let God Fight the Battle:

Our heavenly Father,
Free us of any pride that might hinder us from asking others for the much-needed freedom of forgiveness.
We ask that any wrongdoings or animosity in our hearts we unknowingly harbor toward others be revealed. Let us see those who have wronged us in a new light, pleasing to Your glory, as we remove the grudges and go forward in life.
Soften our hearts to see the good in others where anger and bitterness have held us captive, stopping us from living the life You have chosen for us.
Please help us to become quick to forgive and slow to anger. Allow the forgiveness You

give us to flow from our hearts to the hearts of others. In the holy name of Jesus, we pray,
Amen.

Chapter Ten
What Is Truth?

"The truth always frees us from the self-imposed shackles of lies found in worldly desires."

When asked to define truth, the most common response is "an accurate statement of the facts." For years, this textbook definition of truth was the only one that ever sprang to mind. However, the definition of truth has a much broader concept than the credibility of our assertions.

Life can sometimes be complicated and confusing, causing us to hesitate or feel unsure about our decisions. What if we knew which decisions to make beforehand that would always be in our favor? That kind of insight would save precious time and keep us from making regretful mistakes.

The irony is that we've been given the perfect solution to every challenge in life, yet we sometimes choose a different path. Woven throughout the pages of Scripture are passages that challenge us to consider the implications of our thoughts and actions and how they influence the success or failure of our lives.

One of my favorite passages that left an unforgettable tug on my heart and led me to the truth, found at the foot of the cross, is found in the Gospel of John. Pontius Pilate, the Roman governor who sentenced Jesus to death, questioned Jesus about the truth.

> *Pilate said to Him, "What is truth?" and when he had said this, he went out again to the Jews and said to them, "I find no guilt in Him. (John 18:38)*

Pontius Pilot's question was inspired by a comment made by Jesus earlier in their conversation.

> *Therefore Pilate said to Him, "So You are a king?" Jesus answered, "You say correctly that I am a king. For this I have been born, and for this I have come into the world, to testify to the truth. Everyone who is of the truth hears My voice." (John 18:37)*

When I first read this Scripture, I was far from living a godly life, having experienced three failed marriages, strained family relationships, and a struggle with alcohol abuse. I was aching for the truth to emerge and give hope to a life that seemed to be falling apart more each day.

We might assume we know the way to lasting happiness, but we're often deceived as we fuel our fleshly desires. When our temporary fulfillment fails us, we're left to pick up the pieces of a regrettable deception that remains ingrained in our memories. The truth can only be found in Jesus and what He represents, molded by the Spirit of God.

> *But the fruit of the Spirit is love, joy, peace, patience, kindness, goodness, faithfulness, gentleness, self-control; against such things there is no law. (Galatians 5:22–23)*

Walking in the flesh, often known as the path of deception, refers to our sinful attraction to quick fixes that produce temporary satisfaction. This worldly lifestyle leads to undesirable behavior and self-destructive actions, which undermine our relationships.

> *Now the deeds of the flesh are evident, which are: immorality, impurity, sensuality, idolatry, sorcery, enmities, strife, jealousy, out-*

> *bursts of anger, disputes, dissensions, factions, envying, drunkenness, carousing, and things like these, of which I forewarn you, just as I have forewarned you, that those who practice such things will not inherit the kingdom of God. (Galatians 5:19–21)*

It's all too tempting to succumb to a seductive web of pleasures designed to ease daily stress or enhance our relationships. For instance, a couple begins partaking in a relaxing drink to wind down the day. At first, the thrill of the shared activity and the alcohol loosening the tension of the daily grind is welcome. All seems well.

Over time, the interaction intended to strengthen the connection becomes a source of dread, resulting in conflict and days of silence from harshly spoken words or hurtful behavior. One or both may begin underperforming at work or calling in sick, putting a financial strain on the partnership. A once-welcome event has become a source of contention, with blame placed on each other rather than the source—alcohol.

I'm not suggesting that we should never have an occasional drink to unwind, but rather illustrating how relying on worldly approaches to strengthen the connection can lead to issues. We should never play with fire, thinking we won't get burned. If the potential exists—be careful or avoid the practice.

> *Jesus said to him, "I am the way, and the truth, and the life; no one comes to the Father but through Me." (John 14:6)*

Allowing the Spirit to Work in Our Lives:

With all of the positive aspects of the Spirit, it's obvious why it unmistakably outweighs the detrimental ways of the flesh. The vices and practices of this fallen world only work to sever our bonds, whereas the virtues of the Spirit help reinforce the foundations of our relationships.

It can be difficult to embrace the virtues that strengthen us, yet God gives a solution for our weakness. By adopting Jesus into our lives and following His teachings, we develop the elements that help to change our self-destructive personality. As a helper, the Holy Spirit is sent to us.

> *But the Helper, the Holy Spirit, whom the Father will send in My name, He will teach you all things, and bring to your remembrance all that I said to you. (John 14:26)*

He becomes our best friend and spiritual father, constantly directing us away from the hazardous behaviors produced by our thoughts, words, and actions. It could be a subtle whisper or something meant to grab our attention, such as an insightful conversation, an article that speaks to us, or even a billboard with a message.

The Holy Spirit will also clarify the parts of the Bible that we're having difficulty understanding to help reveal our life's purpose as it unfolds. The closer our relationship with God, the more the Holy Spirit can accomplish in our lives.

A sermon I once heard by Dr. Tony Evans summed it up best. He stated we haven't sincerely invited Jesus into our house simply because we put a sign in the window saying, "Jesus lives here." We must have an unrestricted and open relationship with Him.

Dr. Evans' sermon made complete sense. When we welcome someone into our home, we often use the standard cordial invitation, "Come on in and make yourself at home." Is that what we're truly implying? Not really—in reality, we want them to feel at ease in the spaces we grant them immediate access.

We play it safe and tend to only let people into the parts of our lives where there's no clutter hiding. We can't ask Jesus into our lives, hoping for Him to change our lives, and then tell Him not to enter an area—He can't be a confined guest.

To experience real change, we must give God complete freedom to work in all aspects of our lives. Our helper, the Holy Spirit, will seek to strengthen nine areas that will improve us as individuals, thus improving our relationships. We begin with love.

A Spirit of Love:

When we fall in love with someone, we typically vocalize our feelings at some point. Love, however, entails more than merely telling someone how we feel. It involves consistently showing and making them feel valued at all times and in all things—a spirit of love.

Remember, love is an action word that needs our participation. Love remains merely a descriptive word for our happy emotions if we only talk and do not show—it must have action. It must drive the other characteristics of the Spirit—joy, peace, patience, kindness, goodness, faithfulness, gentleness, and self-control—all elements of a successful relationship.

> *Little children, let us not love with word or with tongue, but in deed and truth. (1 John 3:18)*

A Spirit of Joy:

Joy is a fruit of the Spirit manifested through our obedience to living faithfully by the life-altering teachings of Jesus. The serenity gained through our commitment will produce relational stability and hope, knowing God is our shield of protection.

> *Now may the God of hope fill you with all joy and peace in believing, so that you will abound in hope by the power of the Holy Spirit. (Romans 15:13)*

A Spirit of Peace:

Our daily lives can present numerous obstacles, robbing us of joy. Sometimes, we solve one problem just in time for another to arise. Finding a moment of peace can seem impossible. Life, as we must experience it, will continuously present challenges, but we'll find peace if we remain devoted to Jesus' teachings. The overwhelming moments are conquered by remembering where our strength and hope originate—the truth of God.

When we restore ourselves on the foundation of His Word and the guidance of the Spirit, peace and joy return to our lives, along with renewed hope for a perfect outcome in all we do. We must always remain faithful to the truth.

> *Now may the Lord of peace Himself continually grant you peace in every circumstance. The Lord be with you all! (2 Thessalonians 3:16)*

A Spirit of Patience:

Without the fruit of patience, dealing with anything life throws at us—or each other becomes challenging. Patience is the foundation of all successful relationships and enables us to maintain peace and harmony with the people in our lives.

Patience, along with kindness, is also one of the first defining qualities of our personality. We all know that we'll need to be shown patience at some point, so it becomes a quality we instinctively seek as a prerequisite before initiating a relationship. It holds together all we do—the glue of life.

> *So, as those who have been chosen of God, holy and beloved, put on a heart of compassion, kindness, humility, gentleness and patience; bearing with one another, and forgiving each other, whoever has a complaint against anyone; just as the Lord forgave you, so also should you. Beyond all these things put on love, which is the perfect bond of unity. (Colossians 3:12–14)*

A Spirit of Kindness:

We often hear someone who esteems another person say, "They're so patient and kind." When meeting or reflecting on someone's character, these are the two most desirable attributes that come to mind. Kindness and patience act in tandem as the compassionate duet of a prospective partner's personality that's noticeable.

Showing kindness can be as simple as opening a door or helping with something heavy. Their helpful nature quickly captures our attention in our time of need. Most often, what follows the good deed is the exchange of names and brief conversations that may lead to getting to know one another better.

Consistent kindness is also the quickest approach to mending a damaged relationship. Will everyone return our kindness as we journey through life? No, but God will reward our attempts.

> *but I say unto you, love your enemies, and pray for those who persecute you, so that you may prove yourselves to be sons of your Father who is in heaven; for He causes His sun to rise on the evil and the good, and sends rain on the righteous and the unrighteous. (Matthew 5:44–45)*

A Spirit of Goodness:

When we engage with others, our actions reveal a lot about us without ever having a conversation. When we offer our seat, open a door, let others go ahead of us, or do anything that's considerate to help someone, it's considered an act of kindness. Goodness, on the other hand, is when we do the right thing. Our integrity and morals are the basic elements that define our goodness.

In other words, do we make a habit of doing the right thing even when it's not favorable or easy? The one quality in a person that shines above all others when we think of a good person is their ability to forgive. Forgiveness is the cornerstone of all the outstanding attributes that come with a well-deserved reputation as a virtuous person. Our good nature's defining characteristics serve as a constant reminder to others of who we are at times when we most need it.

Become the person with a reputation of goodness—a beacon of hope for others. The person our partner can't live without.

> *"You are the light of the world. A city set on a hill cannot be hidden; nor does anyone light a lamp and put it under a basket, but on the lampstand, and it gives light to all who are in the house. Let your light shine before men in such a way that they may see your good works, and glorify your*

Father who is in heaven."
(Matthew 5:14–16)

A Spirit of Faithfulness:

When we trust in God, our faith grows as He consistently reveals that He will be there for us when needed. This peace of mind we feel in our relationships is measured in the same way that our faith in God grows—from previous experiences.

When we do what we say or are responsible to the best of our abilities, we maintain trust within our relationships. For example, if we're in charge of paying the electric bill, our spouse is counting on it being paid. Coming home to a dark house will do nothing to win their trust.

If we neglect to pay the electric bill once, it could be regarded as an oversight. However, our continuous neglect of responsibilities will begin to compromise our dependability. We must have confidence in our partners, knowing they share equal responsibility for the relationship dynamics—the Spirit of faithfulness that will never leave us in the dark.

for we walk by faith, not by sight. (2 Corinthians 5:7)

A Spirit of Gentleness:

The wild horse is powerful, tall, and swift, cutting through the wind as it runs free, unchallenged in its natural environment. However, with love, patience, and persistence, it can be tamed. Although domesticated, the wild horse remains the same intimidating beast but has learned to demonstrate gentleness via self-control.

Jesus, with all His divine power, always exhibited self-control. He consistently demonstrated how to love with gentleness, kindness, and humility, which unite rather than aggressiveness that divides us.

A gentle demeanor toward others doesn't imply weakness but rather a proactive, loving heart. Through self-control, our partners will perceive us as a source of strength and refuge—a Spirit of gentleness.

> *"Take My yoke upon you and learn from Me, for I am gentle and humble in heart, and you will find rest for your souls. For My yoke is easy and My burden is light." (Matthew 11:29–30)*

A Spirit of Self-Control:

Our ability to handle negative emotions during stressful circumstances demonstrates our level of self-control. When confronted with a potential conflict, our immediate reactions will either aggravate or de-escalate the situation.

To be successful in sustaining harmony and unity in our relationships, we must learn how to harness the power of the peacemaker in all situations. This is accomplished by allowing the Holy Spirit to guide us in awareness to distinguish which reactions promote unity—a Spirit of self-control. Peacemakers proactively ask themselves, "Does it really matter, and if so, how can we both be at peace through mutual agreement?"

> *A gentle answer turns away wrath, But a harsh word stirs up anger. The tongue of the wise makes knowledge acceptable, but the mouth of fools spouts folly. (Proverbs 15:1–2)*

Always Tell the Truth:

Now that we've discussed the fruit of the Spirit and the teachings of Jesus as the truth, let's look at the traditional definition—don't lie. In the ninth grade, I fabricated a story that imparted a valuable lesson I would never forget.

Because of my father's health, my parents supplemented their income by refurbishing houses, requiring us to relocate often. During one of the restorations, we lived in a run-down neighborhood that I knew my friends would probably mock. Hoping to avoid ridicule, I fabricated a story of living in an upscale neighborhood on the other side of town. To protect my secret, I never invited my friends to visit, claiming I was busy, grounded, or wouldn't be home. It became an endless cycle of telling more lies to protect the initial deception—I was always on guard.

As fate would have it, one day, my friends were riding their bicycles in the neighborhood while I was mowing the grass. I tried to slip around to the back of the house unnoticed. It was too late—they'd spotted me and raced over to where I was standing in shock. The question that followed their greeting ended my long-running falsehood. "Whose grass are you cutting? I thought you lived on the other side of town?" they asked in confusion. For a brief moment, I couldn't find the words—knowing my deception had ended, slowly, I began to explain.

That summer day, I experienced what all liars do when caught—shame. I should've told my friends the truth from the start. Lesson learned—always tell the truth and be yourself. A lie told is a truth denied.

Final Thoughts:

In the secular world, the concept of truth has been diluted and distorted to the point where God, the only truth, is gradually being withdrawn from our lives. More than ever, society seeks ways to remove anything goldy and replace it with the worldly practices eroding the family values and virtues that successful relationships depend on and thrive.

Many churches today even shamefully accommodate sin to avoid offending anyone. Well, God is offended, and He's the goodness in our homes and the classroom that we seek to remove. Is it surprising that our society and relationships disintegrate when God isn't the glue? How can we expect anything good if we build on the sands of deception that will inevitably fail?

> *And the rain fell, and the floods came, and the winds blew and slammed against that house; and yet it did not fall, for it had been founded on the rock. Everyone who hears these words of Mine and does not act on them, will be like a foolish man who built his house on the sand. The rain fell, and the floods came, and the winds blew and slammed against that house; and it fell—and great was its fall. (Matthew 7:25-27)*

One of the biggest problems in modern culture is the reliance on secular methods to solve a spiritual problem. We must have complete faith in Jesus' teachings, clinging to the foundation He has laid, or succumb to deception and defeat.

> *For no one can lay any foundation other than the one we already have—Jesus Christ.*
> *(1 Corinthians 3:11)*

When the storms and seasons of our relationship pass, love and truth will endure and be remembered. They will become our anchor as we hold on to our increased faith in God and one another. As we grow in the Spirit, we'll grow in unity and become more connected with God, our rock, the third person in our chord of three. *(Ecclesiastes 4:12)* We will walk in the truth, knowing which path will contribute to the well-being of our relationship.

> *Then Jesus again spoke to them, saying, "I am the Light of the world; the one who follows Me will not walk in the darkness, but will have the Light of life." (John 8:12)*

Strategy for Success:

- Truth is living by the teachings of Jesus.

- Allow Jesus an open and unrestrained invitation into our lives.

- Let our goodness be the reputation that defines us to others.

- Patience is the foundation of all positive virtues and the foundation of self-control.

- Use the TWA filter method to help manage our self-control.

- Let our statements be accurate so we live free from the bondage of lies.

- Living by the desires of the flesh is to build a house on sand. It never lasts.

Related Scripture:

- *1 John 3:18*

- *1 John 17:17*

- *Psalm 86:11*

- *Ephesians 4:15*

- *John 8:31–32*

Let God Fight the Battle:

*Father of Truth in Heaven,
Help us grow in Your spirit of
truth in all things.
Lord, grant us the courage
to live and speak Your truth,
even when it's hard.
We ask that the fruit of
the Spirit be evident in our
thoughts, words, and actions.
Lord, we give You the things
we can't control or fix without
Your guidance.
We ask only to glorify You in
all we do.
In the name of Jesus,
Amen.*

Chapter Eleven

THE ARMORED CONNECTION

"If we want to protect others, we should first seek to protect them from ourselves."

The enemy, Satan, will attack us with endless temptations and obstacles to undo the gains we've accomplished as our bond of love grows. Why? Because he despises humanity, and his ultimate objective is to destroy us because of his contempt for God.

> *The thief comes only to steal and kill and destroy; I came so that they would have life, and have it abundantly. (John 10:10)*

We all want to believe we do everything possible to keep our loved ones safe. But are we really protecting them from all potential threats? Our misconceptions of protection may lead to insufficient safeguards, putting ourselves and our relationships at risk.

Unknowingly, we often overlook the most subtle, catastrophic, and pervasive threat—the spiritual attack. Some of the physical attacks we suffer can be healed over time, but spiritual attacks can permanently harm our mental well-being.

> *for bodily discipline is only of little profit, but godliness is profitable for all things, since it holds promise for the present life and also for the life to come. (1 Timothy 4:8)*

From God's Perspective:

Love—*always protects*

> *Pull me from the trap my enemies set for me, for I find protection in you alone. (Psalms 31:4)*

From Vice to Virtue:

A plant will thrive if planted in the warmth of the sun, nourished in healthy soil, and shielded from harsh elements. Like plants, we must nurture and protect our budding relationships from an environment hostile to healthy growth and survival. We must also eradicate any encroaching "weeds."

A weed is anything that has the potential to undermine the success of the relationship. At first, some of the weeds that enter our lives may appear harmless and innocent. However, if permitted to share space, they deplete the vitality of the relationship and poison the fertile soil that sustains our healthy relational well-being.

> *Therefore, since we have so great a cloud of witnesses surrounding us, let us also lay aside every encumbrance and the sin which so easily entangles us, and let us run with endurance the race that is set before us. (Hebrews 12:1)*

We begin protecting our relationships by identifying the areas of potential attack. The following are the most common spiritual targets for "weed" infiltration:

- Relationship secrets

- Transparent associations

- Relationship time management

- Personal time management
- Parenting
- Our testimony
- Private issues
- Friends

Relationship Secrets:

A secret is a damaging "weed" with the potential to undermine or destroy the relationship's trust—a time bomb, ready to ignite. When secrets are revealed, and they usually are, the relationship's connection suffers, requiring us to devote time and effort to restoring our trustworthiness.

The best strategy to preserve the relationship's integrity is maintaining open, honest communication that leaves nothing intentionally hidden. If we've been concealing a secret, to protect the relationship, we come clean with our partner and end the cycle of deception. Remember, it's easier to address a single deception than multiple lies created to cover up the original offense.

> *Truthful lips will endure forever, but a lying tongue is only for a moment. (Proverbs 12:19)*

Transparent Associations:

Years ago, a friend shared his story about a seemingly harmless interaction with a long-time acquaintance of the opposite sex. They had known each other since high school, where they became good friends before going to the same community and state college campuses. Surprisingly, after graduation, they found jobs near each other, making an occasional lunch together convenient.

One day, a mutual friend of the couple was shopping and witnessed their luncheons. She immediately called to inform her friend of what she had observed. Despite the friendship's innocence, suspicion emerged as a "weed" in the once-trustworthy marriage due to the reluctance to bring awareness of the lunch with a friend.

Transparency about the friendship would've spared a lot of confusion, potential conflict, and damaged relational trust. We may argue that the wife suffers from jealousy and that it's socially acceptable to eat lunch with the opposite gender. While it may be acceptable, these social misunderstandings invite problems into the relationship. What one person may regard as a harmless meal with a friend, another may consider an intimate lunch date.

If my friend had taken a straightforward and honest approach, he could have avoided any unexpected misunderstanding. He should have told his wife about his friend and invited her to dinner or an activity to introduce them.

If a couple agrees to have opposite-sex friends, some ground rules should be followed. First, always limit physical touch—if you wouldn't touch a relative that way, it's probably inappropriate with a friend.

Second, remember that relational issues are sacred and confidential, only to be shared with God in prayer and a counselor for therapy. It's tempting to want to vent to someone for validation or support, but be wary of the consequences. Relatives and friends are known to offer advice that supports their personal objectives and marital dynamics but may not be in our best interests. Proceed with caution.

Talking with others about our marital issues can also lead to trust issues. If our partner struggles to communicate openly and we betray that trust, they may stop sharing altogether. Never let others advocate our futures—submit our problems to God, the sole third person and divine counselor in our marriage, and wait for the results.

I'm not asserting that we shouldn't have friends of the opposite gender, but we should do so responsibly.

Relationship Time Management:

Finding time for everything deserving of our attention can often feel impossible in today's fast-paced world. As discussed earlier, we can better organize our lives by following the 60/40 guidelines to help prioritize our schedules.

If you recall, the 60/40 prioritization method entails devoting a percentage of our time to the needed areas, understanding that modifications may be necessary.

Time spent with the person we love is the heartbeat that keeps the relationship alive and yields the lifelong memories that endear us—make the time, never letting the weeds infiltrate our solid foundation.

> *for where your treasure is,*
> *there your heart will be also.*
> *(Matthew 6:21)*

Personal Time Management:

Although we must make time for our relationships, we must also make time for ourselves. We must never lose focus on our personal goals, hobbies, and other interests—who we are. If we lose our individuality, we cannot give our spouse the person they fell in love with—we can't give what we no longer have.

While we wed to become one, we must always listen to our hearts and employ our individual God-given talents. Our individualism is meant to strengthen the unity of the relational bond and help us fulfill the task that God has given us—our calling.

> *so we, who are many, are one*
> *body in Christ, and individ-*
> *ually parts of one another.*
> *(Romans 12:5)*

Throughout His ministry, the Lord was continually healing and caring for others, yet He still made time for Himself. Jesus would occasionally leave the crowds to rest and pray alone, demonstrating how we should care for ourselves. He even went to a wedding and, while there, turned water into wine. *(John 2:1–11)*

By making time for ourselves, we minimize the tension arising from our everyday struggles and responsibilities that can spill over into our relationships. Weeds can be prevented by living a well-rounded existence and staying loyal to who God designed us to be and with whom our spouse first fell in love.

As we grow as individuals, our relationships inherently evolve as a collective effort—everyone benefits.

> *The second is this, you shall love your neighbor as yourself. There is no other commandments greater than these. (Mark 12:31)*

Parenting:

Parenting is one of the most common sources of conflict in a relationship. The mold we were born and poured into, shaped by our parents and life experiences, can collide with the ideals of our partners as we try to instill our upbringing in our children. Before seeking to become parents, we should first talk about how we intend to raise our children and reach a mutual understanding.

If we fail to reach an acceptable compromise and one parent begins to make decisions for the children on their own, resentment can emerge, resulting in tension. In time, the children will also become aware of the split decision-making and seek out the parent who responds most favorably. The problem compounds.

Is it necessary for both parents to always be involved in every minor decision? Of course not. However, if a child asks a question that may necessitate a joint decision, always wait until it's discussed with our partner. We navigate questions of this nature by simply explaining to our child that the question will be discussed by both parents, and they will be informed of the decision at a later time. Never leave an open door for division when parenting.

> *If a house is divided against itself, that house will not be able to stand. (Mark 3:25)*

Our Testimony:

I've always believed that God arranges for us to be in the right place at the right time to say the words that can change someone's life. Billy Graham devoted his life to Jesus after attending a tent revival and hearing a traveling preacher's sermon.

What if that preacher had a tarnished reputation as a result of misinformation? Would Billy have been receptive to his sermon, or would he have turned his back on the life-changing message? Is it possible that Billy's redemption wouldn't have occurred that day?

Billy Graham went on to travel the world, speaking words that altered the lives of millions. God had planned for that specific preacher to be in that exact location, at that time, and date. We all have a divine purpose and must protect one another from false rumors that tarnish how others perceive us.

We must be confident, knowing that our spouse will defend our good name if necessary—together, we're a powerful team that God can bless as He uses our testimony.

> *But I tell you that every careless word that people speak, they shall give an accounting for it in the day of judgment. For by your words you will be justified, and by your words you will be condemned. (Matthew 12:36–37)*

Private Issues:

As discussed earlier, relationship issues are private unless for the purpose of consulting with a marriage counselor. Scripture encourages us to confess our sins to one another rather than to anybody who would listen. Once a secret is revealed, the damage is sometimes irreversible.

> *Argue your case with your neighbor, and do not reveal the secret of another, or one*

> *who hears it will put you to shame, And the evil report about you will not pass away.*
> *(Proverbs 25:9–10)*

As previously stated, we must be cautious when confiding in family, friends, or coworkers. Avoiding the practice entirely is the best approach while working through issues. Why? Because their concern for us can cause them to give poor and biased counsel.

Assume we tell a sibling our spouse is upset because we purchased something without informing them. What typically follows is something like, "I wouldn't tolerate that. You should be free to spend as much money as you like. It's your money also."

However, we failed to inform our sibling of our habitual overspending on frivolous items, jeopardizing the family budget. Unfortunately, an unjust opinion of our spouse may be formed, impacting relationships with other family members. The financial issue remains and is now empowered to worsen—great job, sibling.

Distorted advice may also come from someone who has been through or is going through the same scenario but has yet to heal. A vendetta, we could say. Suppose we're dealing with an unfaithful spouse, and in our anguish, we seek advice from someone suffering from infidelity—their input will probably be tainted.

If we need relationship advice, we should consult a Christian counselor or someone with no stake in the outcome. We deserve unbiased, untainted truth when seeking solutions to the obstacles that will affect us and our lives. The best counseling will always come from above, through prayer.

> *I will instruct you and teach you in the way which you should go; I will advise you with My eye upon you.*
> *(Psalm 32:8)*

Friends:

The typical friend or acquaintance gives us a sense of belonging, someone to share mutual interests and offer comfort and support in times of need. A heartfelt friendship, on the other hand, goes beyond the typical buddy or companion concept. This special individual will protect and contribute to our overall well-being in every way.

I've heard it said we can count our true friends on one hand. Through the years, I've come to see the wisdom in that old adage. A sincere friend will boldly speak what we need but don't want to hear, preventing us from compromising or undermining our values. They encourage us to improve our lives, helping us be our best. They protect us from ourselves.

A devoted friend will never encourage us to do anything that jeopardizes our health, testimony, families, careers, or relationships with others. Unfortunately, some of our associates or so-called friends may not consider the consequences of engaging in behaviors that endanger our relationship.

If compromising activities make it difficult to maintain a friendship, we should express our concerns to them. Inform them that while we value their friendship, our marriage is the top priority, and we need their understanding and support.

Make no compromises that will devalue the relationship with our spouse. If they continue to reject our convictions, it may be necessary to discontinue the association. We must always prioritize our partner and the relationship.

True friends, the kind you can count on one hand, will recognize the importance of our relationship and not be offended by our spouse being the primary focus. They will promote the solid virtues we should all live by in our pursuit of happiness. Wisdom—make it a habit to choose our friends wisely.

> *A person of too many friends comes to ruin, but there is a friend who sticks closer than a brother. (Proverbs 18:24)*

The Role God Has Defined for Husbands:

When I first became a Christian, I was aware of my leadership role in the family, but I had concerns if I could carry it out as God intended. I began listening to sermons, reading relationship books, and studying Scripture about marriage and the role of a spiritual leader.

Still, I couldn't stop the thoughts of failure from manifesting. Will Shelah honor my leadership? Will she let me be the deciding factor if we disagree? Is it possible for me to fulfill this responsibility without disappointing her or God?

My answers came after much prayer—everything is in God's control, and I need only to persist in the role assigned to me. There will be days when we're appreciated and loved for our efforts, as well as days of being judged, resented, and questioned. During these times, keep focused on God as our guide—it's a validation that we're on the right track and is usually followed by a spiritual attack on the relationship. The relationship will enter a cycle of conflict, and we must believe that God will reward our efforts with victory and forgive our shortcomings.

> *So humble yourselves under the mighty power of God, and at the right time he will lift you up in honor. Give all your worries and cares to God, for he cares about you. (1 Peter 5:6–7)*

If we feel ourselves or our partners straying from God's will, we encourage change with love, patience, and the power of prayer. Remember, God has the power to change others—not us. There are three crucial fundamental factors to remember as we progress in the function:

1. Be a strong leader, not a weak boss. Our role doesn't change our partner being our equal.

2. Learn together. Refrain from pretending to have all the answers.

3. Accept that only God can change people.

When unsure how to manage a relational challenge, we must refrain from being too hard on ourselves. During these times, remain in prayer, allow the Holy Spirit to guide, and offer unwavering love and patience until the issue is resolved.

> *Husbands, love your wives, just as Christ also loved the church and gave Himself up for her, so that He might sanctify her, having cleansed her by the washing of water with the word, that He might present to Himself the church in all her glory, having no spot or wrinkle or any such thing; but that she would be holy and blameless. So husbands ought also to love their own wives as their own bodies. He who loves his own wife loves himself; for no one ever hated his own flesh, but nourishes and cherishes it, just as Christ also does the church. (Ephesians 5:25–29)*

A comforting thought to remember—God never gives us an assignment without the resources to accomplish the task. Now for the ladies' role in the relationship.

The Role God Has Defined for Wifes:

Before we proceed, I want to be clear on the role of men in a marriage. Husbands, as spiritual leaders, we aren't granted the right to demand our wives to be at our beck and call. It simply implies that we follow Christ's spiritual example as the head of the church.

As husbands, we give Christ sovereignty over ourselves, and the wife, in turn, should give the husband spiritual authority over her—as long as he is guided by the Word of God. The wife's godly function in the relationship is critical. Her role is to be the helper in the relationship, contributing to the success of the husband to become who God has designed him to be in life.

> *Wives, be subject to your own husbands, as to the Lord. For the husband is the head of the wife, as Christ also is the head of the church, He Himself being the Savior of the body. But as the church is subject to Christ, so also the wives ought to be to their husbands in everything. (Ephesians 5:22–24)*

She also plans and oversees household administration. Husbands, it's vital to respect our wives' homemaking decisions and value the emotional stability they contribute to the family dynamics. Without them, we would lack the glue that ties the family together. Trust me, most guys fail to have this talent. One of the many blessings I take for granted is Shelah's candor and readiness to correct me on a matter if needed.

I sometimes allow my pride to get in the way of her correction at times, but I always think about our conversation and strive for change as the Spirit smacks me on the head, helping me see the error of my ways. Shelah is the glue in our family, for sure. I'm thankful for her role—she does it well.

> *so that they may encourage the young women to love their husbands, to love their children, to be sensible, pure, workers at home, kind, being subject to their own husbands, so that the word of God will not be dishonored. (Titus 2: 4–5)*

The Two Become One:

Even though we have defined functions in the relationship, we're still a team and should support one another in our roles. As we collaborate to fulfill our obligations. we learn about what motivates the emotional components and perspectives of the genders.

Dr. Tony Evans once gave a sermon that emphasized best what the husband and wife needed emotionally from each other. A wife provides her husband respect by elevating his mind, while a husband secures her heart with committed and expressed love. As always, Scripture points to the path that will help us to fulfill our roles and protect our relationships from the "weeds"—love and respect.

> *Nevertheless, as for you individually, each husband is to love his own wife the same as himself, and the wife must see to it that she respects her husband. (Ephesians 5:33)*

Final Thoughts:

When our relationship is in trouble, our first defense should be always to seek God. He created us, the concept of love, and relationships, making Him the supreme authority and knowing us better than anyone else. His flawless answers will never lead us astray, providing a perfect solution to our confusion. It can be tempting at times to end a relationship that continues to bring us pain and suffering, but if we feel the relationship is worthy of our love—we fight.

I continuously pray for God to bless my relationship, even though I make constant mistakes. I will never have the capability to become the perfect husband. Despite this, with God's grace, I have the means to be as close to perfect as possible to be the partner Shelah needs and deserves. I have much work on myself to be pleasing by God's perfect standards, but I keep running after that goal, keeping my eyes focused on Him, knowing that I'm a work in progress.

The more we put our faith in God, the stronger the divine protection of the relationship—we build an armor that will protect us from whatever "weeds" we encounter.

> *You are from God, little children, and have overcome them; because greater is He who is in you than he who is in the world. (1 John 4:4)*

Strategy for Success:

- When "weeds" appear—remove them.
- Successful relationships have no secrets.
- Always prioritize the relationship.
- Always parent together.
- Always protect our spouse's testimony.

- Keep relational issues private.

- Be cautious of advice from friends and family.

- Choose friends that are relationship-friendly.

Related Scripture:

- *Galatians 6:1–2*

- *2 Thessalonians 3:3*

- *James 4:7*

- *Romans 15:1*

- *James 5:19–20*

Let God Fight the Battle:

> *Lord,*
> *Protect us from the evil one that seeks only to destroy our relationships.*
> *Teach us to safeguard our paths in life through complete faith in Your divine plan.*
> *May we always stand on the*

rock of Your love and protection.

Lord, strengthen our love to establish a bond that will endure the storms.

By the protection, found in the name of Jesus, we ask these things,
Amen.

Chapter Twelve

TRUST WITHOUT RUST

"Our trust, like iron, can withstand enormous weight, but if constantly exposed to corrosive elements, rust can form, weakening its once-reliable strength—it becomes untrustworthy."

Trustworthiness is often associated with being a faithful spouse, demonstrating competence, and keeping one's promises. When we blend these trust representations, we foster a sense of security that helps to preserve the integrity of the relationship—a culture of trust that can be built upon.

For example, picture an interview where a law enforcement officer questions a suspect. If the suspect begins the interview dishonestly, would the officer be likely to believe the credibility of follow-up questions? However, if the suspect begins the interrogation with credible replies, the officer is prone to trust their story.

Now that we've gotten a sense of what trust is, let's talk about when we need it to function in the best interests of both partners. You've probably heard the phrase, "Trust must be earned." The problem with that logic is that if we begin a relationship distrusting, we play the roles of judge, juror, and executioner towards a possibly innocent person.

Remember, we're only guilty when the evidence proves that we committed a crime, not before. So, doesn't it make more sense to freely establish trust when meeting someone rather than forcing them to prove themselves?

In my teens, I dated a girl who'd been the victim of unfaithfulness with deep emotional scars that led her to assume that all guys are disloyal. I constantly felt the repercussions of this previous act, even though I had nothing to do with her painful experience.

For her to feel secure, I could only hang out with mutual friends, so she felt our relationship was safeguarded. It would upset her even more if I didn't answer the phone when she called. It became too much to manage, so we stopped dating.

I can't emphasize this enough—wait until an infraction has occurred to avoid unnecessary tension, distance, and uncomfortable feelings—for both partners. If we make a habit of prejudging and making someone earn our trust, we may push them away and miss out on getting to know some wonderful people.

> *"Do not judge, and you will not be judged; and do not condemn, and you will not be condemned; pardon, and*

you will be pardoned." (Luke 6:37)

If we've ever been the victim of betrayal, we need to heal before embarking on a new relationship. If not, emotional pain may still be lingering in our thoughts, having the potential to impact our behavior. We must always give ourselves time to heal from any emotional distress that could contribute to unreasonable and unfair thoughts or acts toward others. We should always take the time to recover and sort our emotions to be fair to ourselves and our next partner.

To begin the healing process, we must determine if we're feeling anger, resentment, depression, grief, or a combination of these emotions. If we're experiencing several emotions, we should address one problem at a time until our feelings are no longer triggered. Be patient—unforgiven or unresolved emotions can reemerge, wreaking havoc on our relationships. Get it right.

If we've been the perpetrators of mistrust in our current relationship, we must accept that our partner will need time to heal. It's understandable to try to restore trust as soon as possible, but avoid premature fixes or exaggerated efforts—they will usually fail.

Because betrayal makes us feel vulnerable to further harm, it increases paranoia and anxiety—natural self-preservation. During the healing process, be a loyal and understanding partner—in time and with forgiveness, it will be enough to reclaim confidence in the relationship. Be patient, deep wounds take time to heal—go slow.

From God's Perspective:

Love—*always trusts*

> *There is no fear in love, but perfect love casts out fear, because fear involves punishment, and the one who fears is not perfected in love. (1 John 4:18)*

We cannot love someone while living in fear—it only punishes the other person. If we love as God intended, we attain the closest thing to perfect love as flawed beings can achieve, living in the security of His Word.

From Vice to Virtue:

The Bible often tells us to put our faith in God rather than humanity. Is this to say we shouldn't trust others?

> *Thus says the Lord, "Cursed is the man who trusts in mankind and makes flesh his strength, and whose heart turns away from the Lord." (Jeremiah 17:5)*

How can we trust others if we can only trust God? It's a fair question, one that I struggled with for years. There was a time in my life when, because of past experiences, I grew not to trust others.

Over time, I realized that God always engineers a favorable outcome no matter what happens, good or bad. Sometimes, a positive outcome isn't apparent or understood at the time, but things always work out within God's will, which is always in our best interests.

To have faith in people, we must trust God without reservation that He has our back in all circumstances. When there's unconditional trust, the dynamics of our relationships flow like a river, establishing a culture of love and a bond of security.

We must first remove the barriers that impede the development of a trusting atmosphere. In doing so, we establish the groundwork for a healthy, reliable relationship. Some of the obstacles that hinder this positive growth include:

- Confidentiality
- Deflection
- Friends
- Character
- Relational support
- Creates doubt

Confidentiality:

Relationships are supposed to be a safe haven for our personal issues and private information. It should be where we feel secure talking about whatever we want to vent—without the world finding out.

If we violate their privacy, trust suffers, especially if it keeps happening, and they may cease confiding in us or seeking advice, feeling more comfortable dealing with challenges independently rather than relying on our support. If this happens, the relationship starts to regress.

I recall sitting around a bonfire one night when a couple began discussing how their partner avoided talking about their past. It was obvious the discussion wasn't going to end with a deflection of the subject. The heat around the fire suddenly felt hotter.

The partner who brought up the subject just wanted to know more about the person they were in a relationship with—her request made sense. So did the following sentence that was to come out of her partner's mouth.

In a frustrated and on-the-spot tone, he said, "I used to love talking to you about everything until I began feeling like I was telling you, the family, our friends, or anyone that would listen. That's why I stopped talking to you about much of anything private."

The discussion ended with, "Can we talk about this when we get home?"

Privacy had been invaded, and relational trust had become the cost of the violation. We have no right to tell others about our partner's past or to divulge sensitive or emotional issues without their consent—ever. Medical practitioners, spiritual leaders, teachers, and counselors are all subject to tight secrecy rules;

can we not recognize the need for trust in our relationships? We don't get to decide what can be discussed in an open forum with others, as certain topics may be off-limits in regard to our partners.

If we believe our partner's previous experiences may benefit someone, we should respectfully ask permission to divulge the information or, even better, for them to speak with the person. Allowing the person who went through the experience to provide their testimony may be more effective in most cases. It's not so much what's said as how it's presented and who says it—power in the delivery.

If we fail to ask permission before disclosing sensitive information, what was intended to help others may only undermine our relationship. We can't expect intimate conversations to become common practice if we abuse our spouse's trust in private matters. This area of the relationship is where we must respect the confidential convictions of the individual.

> *One who goes about as a slanderer reveals secrets, But one who is trustworthy conceals a matter. (Proverbs 11:13)*

Deflection:

Have you ever tried to talk to someone about a concern, only to have them redirect the conversation to something you did in the past? Regrettably, I've used this tactic to avoid discussions when I was annoyed, unwilling to change, or unprepared to deal with the matter. During my drinking days, it became my favorite filibuster. Throughout my struggle with alcohol, other people often served as my justification for drinking. In my displaced thoughts, those denying responsibility for their role in my drinking gave way to more excuses to indulge—a perfect ploy to relieve me of responsibility for my actions.

In reality, it only prolonged the inevitable. When an issue is diverted, constructive and positive energy is channeled toward defending rather than resolving. A total waste of time. The unaddressed problem continues to impact the relationship's wellness and personal growth.

If ignored over an extended period, it could result in even more underlying issues. For instance, if we're the victim of someone diverting problems, we may inadvertently begin accepting and believing everything is our fault to avoid arguing—a form of what is referred to as gaslighting. As a result, we isolate ourselves from our partners, making it difficult for them to feel comfortable talking to us about most topics.

The practice of blaming others has been around for a long time. When God inquired about Adam's involvement in bringing sin into the world, he blamed Eve—the first recorded deflection.

> *Then the Lord God called to the man, and said to him, "Where are you?" He said, "I heard the sound of You in the garden, and I was afraid be-*

> *cause I was naked; so I hide myself." And He said, "Who told you that you were naked? Have you eaten from the tree of which I commanded you not to eat?" The man said, "The woman whom You gave to be with me, she gave me from the tree, and I ate."*
> *(Genesis 3:9–12)*

Friends:

One of the most prominent characteristics of habitually deceitful people is that their social group changes regularly. When I first started driving, a neighbor I mistook for a friend taught me this vital life lesson.

I often invited my neighbor on errands or provided him with transportation when I could. He needed a ride—I loved the company. Over time, I began to notice missing coins from my ashtray or money from the envelope I kept in the glove box for emergencies. I would replenish the funds, only for it to go missing again. One day after dropping him off, I noticed my wallet was missing from its usual resting place in the truck's console. Panic quickly set in from losing my driver's license and the money given to me for my recent birthday. I retraced my every step, searching every possible location, but couldn't locate the wallet.

A few days later, I asked my friend to go with me to town, and as he crawled into the truck, he casually handed me my wallet. I opened it brimming with hope, only to discover that the money given to me for my birthday was missing. He told me, straight-faced, that he found it at a nearby convenience store where we would often stop for gas. Trying to see the positive side of the circumstances, I was relieved to at least get my license back.

As I was backing out of his driveway, his mother rushed out, yelling an incriminating statement, "I'm glad your wallet was found in the driveway last weekend. It fell out of your truck as you got in to leave." My eyebrows wrinkled in confusion as I gazed at my so-called friend, trying to decipher the contradictory stories I'd just been told. After chatting with other neighbors, I discovered they had also been victims of such behavior while he was present. A common denominator was emerging, forcing him to make new connections in other social circles. We never spoke much after the lost wallet episode.

Lesson learned—we should be cautious of those who display a pattern of repeatedly changing social circles for no apparent reason. Although to be realistic, we must also remember that a lack of integrity isn't the only reason a person may change friends. Sometimes, it's for legitimate reasons. As you may recall, my parents moved around refurbishing houses, forcing me to change friends repeatedly.

A person in recovery from substance abuse or criminal history may also wisely seek to avoid former friends who may encourage relapse—an understandable reason to relocate. A career, closer to family, or medical reasons are also valid reasons to make changes or relocate.

Character:

Things aren't always as they appear. Magicians and illusionists frequently use the concept of deception to entertain audiences by fooling them into seeing things that aren't there or making them disappear. Unfortunately, we meet people who perform the same illusionary act in their character.

The deceitfulness we encounter from others typically occurs after settling comfortably into the relationship. For example, we may have dressed more upscale or dressy on our first few dates. After we began feeling comfortable around each other, we relaxed, wearing more casual clothing. This is a normal change and a sign of our increased comfort level around each other—a good thing.

In the same manner, as a person starts to feel comfortable in the relationship, they may reveal negative personality changes previously hidden. When we notice our partners' personalities changing, we should promptly initiate a discovery talk to determine the cause of the sudden change. Note—if an existing problem that requires our support is uncovered, it may not be intentional dishonesty. It could be a delicate topic they're hesitant to share —not intended to be deceiving. When faced with this situation, we must be patient, understanding, and supportive as we unravel the problem.

On the other hand, a person may attempt to conceal negative character flaws, not seeing them as a problem. Toxic people aren't born with personalities that can't be changed through love, patience, and willingness. Sometimes, a person hasn't dealt with the underlying wounds caused by trauma, causing inside pain to radiate outward to others. Whatever the case, once problems are identified, we must address them and seek solutions. While working through the challenges, be patient so that trust develops between both partners as a solution is reached.

It's also crucial not to blame ourselves for failing to see a person's concealed characteristics. Remember, a deceitful person has practiced masking the negative aspects they've hidden longer than we've had experience discovering toxic traits. We can take the time to get to know someone, but we only know what someone reveals. The deceit results from the deceiver, not our failure to exercise caution.

> *The heart is more deceitful than all else and is desperately sick; Who can understand it? (Jeremiah 17:9)*

Relational Support:

We never know what daily challenges life will bring. We may awaken to a day filled with awesome blessings or one we wish we could just skip. Whatever the day presents, we must face it with God's grace, and a little assistance from our partner never hurts.

When our partners are going through a difficult time, they'll appreciate and remember our help with navigating the challenging event. This is the perfect opportunity to assure them they can rely on us and instill trust in our ability to be helpful companions.

During these trying times, we may need to go above and beyond the small acts of kindness that don't take much effort, such as opening a door, taking in the groceries, or freeing a snug jar lid. While such gestures show that we care, our partner may require a more hands-on approach. Until the imminent issue passes, we should utilize the 60/40 support strategy to contribute more to our spouse's needs.

One of the challenges I've struggled with is figuring out how to support someone in the way they need. My initial response was to do little things to free up their time, but it never felt enough, as if I needed to do more. In time and plenty of failed attempts, I began to understand the diverse needs of the individual are key to being a supportive partner. A point to always remember for navigating the dynamics of heartfelt support.

We can fail to provide the support may need because we tend to instinctively help someone the same way we'd prefer in a comparable situation. For example, if a person loves company when sick, that's how we help—our presence. In contrast, if we prefer to be left alone and snuggle up under the covers till our illness passes, that works for us, not our partner. When supporting our partner, help the individual, not the concept.

"How can I help?" is a powerful question that'll reveal how to be a supportive partner. This personalized inquiry ensures that our partners receive the assistance they prefer during their times of need. It makes this trying time of life about them, not us.

> *Do not withhold good from those to whom it is due, when it is in your power to do it. (Proverbs 3:27)*

Creates Doubt:

If we want our spouses to feel a culture of trust surrounding the relationship, the honesty of our words and actions must be consistent. Can we expect someone to believe us if we keep deceiving them or breaking promises?

A consistent pattern of empty words and deeds only gives reason to believe nothing will change or should be expected. If we consistently present our partners with the trustworthy person we all desire, their confidence in the relationship will skyrocket.

> *The one who is faithful in a very little thing is also faithful in much; and the one who is unrighteous in a very little thing is also unrighteous in much. (Luke 16:10)*

Final Thoughts:

Remember that perfect love, God's desire for us, casts out all our worries. Through our faith in God, which establishes our trust in one another, we thrive within a relationship that doesn't punish but grows in lasting love.

> *Therefore, if you are presenting your offering at the altar, and there you remember that your brother has something against you, leave your offering there before the altar and go; first be reconciled to your brother, and then come and present your offering. (Matthew 5:23–24)*

As we can see from the verses above, God would rather we mend a damaged relationship than for us to worship Him. Why? Because we cannot sincerely worship God and bring Him glory while harboring unforgiveness or distrust in our hearts. He takes forgiveness seriously, and we should also.

If the relationship's trust has been compromised, we must swallow our pride and have the difficult conversations that will rekindle the connection. Forgiveness overcomes the hurdles in our pursuit of perfect trust that ushers in a new day, overflowing with hope as we rely on one another in faith.

> *As iron sharpens iron, so one person sharpens another. (Proverbs 27:17)*

Strategy for Success:

- Never make someone earn trust if they haven't proven untrustworthy.

- Resolve any past trust issues before starting a new relationship.

- We build trust by being dependable when our partners need support.

- Always keep our promises, maintaining 100% honesty and openness.

- Secrets in relationships spell disaster.

- Never breach our spouse's confidentiality.

- Accept responsibility by not deflecting blame.

- Try to live by a trustworthy testimony and let it become our resume for others.

- Little things can strengthen or weaken trust—choose what we say or do wisely.

Related Scripture:

- *Proverbs 3:5*

- *Proverbs 31:11*
- *1 John 4:18*
- *1 Corinthians 13:7*
- *Romans 1:12*

Let God Fight the Battle:

> *Heavenly Father,*
> *We trust in Your truth to guide us.*
> *Remove any unvalidated trust concerns that exist within us.*
> *Show us the path when lost in deception and our way is unclear.*
> *Help us swallow our pride and bring all wrongs or secrets to the light to be resolved and forgiven.*
> *Help us cultivate trust in our relationships without fear, as love requires.*
> *Father, we ask these things in*

the name of our Savior, Jesus, Amen.

Chapter Thirteen
I Sure Hope So

"Because of a faithful God that loves us undeservingly, life is worth believing in when all seems hopeless."

As a child facing life's difficulties, my mother would tell me, "I sure hope everything works out. Sending up prayers." I always appreciated her encouraging words but wondered why we couldn't just ask God for what we preferred—victory rather than mere hope.

As I grew older, I realized Mom was teaching me to have a realistic understanding of how life works. We can only pray that everything works out in our favor according to God's will—hope. Faith is knowing that God is working out His flawless plan for us and that we must be patient.

> *Now faith is the assurance of things hoped for, the conviction of things not seen. (Hebrews 11:1)*

During the most challenging period of my life, I began realizing how hope and faith work in unison. In 2018, I was diagnosed with stage three colon cancer. When the physicians delivered the diagnosis, it was as if time had stood still. For a brief moment, I felt an emptiness, as if my body were just a shell incapable of producing a thought. Suddenly, a sensation of peace filled me, and I calmly asked the medical staff, "What do I need to do?" I wasn't sure if I was up for the battle of my lifetime, but one thing was for sure—I knew God was.

After leaving the doctor's office, I felt compelled to go home and read my Bible in hopes of finding some comfort. A verse I read inspired and empowered me to face the challenges ahead.

> *For to me, to live is Christ and to die is gain. But if I am to live on in the flesh, this will mean fruitful labor for me; and I do not know which to choose. But I am hard-pressed from both directions, having the desire to depart and be with Christ, for that is very much better; yet to remain on in the flesh is more necessary for your sake. (Philippians 1:21–24)*

It has always astounded me how God meets our needs at just the right time. After reading the encouraging message found in the Philippians passage, I had a stronger sense of oneness with God. His message came through loud and clear. For once in my life, I was in a win-win situation. My optimistic hope had turned into a solid faith in God. If I survived cancer, it would verify that God had a plan for me. If I didn't prevail against the disease—I would still win.

In the days ahead, the first priority when waking would be to thank God for another day, which I still practice. One grateful morning, I had an appointment with the oncology team to review my initial treatment strategy. After arriving for the appointment and waiting for what seemed like forever—boredom crept into my mind.

I began to gaze out the hospital window at the bumper-to-bumper traffic as the sound of blaring horns sent their impatient message. The longer I watched, the more it reminded me of the frantic life of an ant—a comparison to humanity's hurriedness. How chaotic our daily lives have become as we scurry around fulfilling the daily grind we call life.

My thoughts returned to the waiting area, and I noticed that a companion accompanied some patients while others were alone. I realized how much people dealing with cancer rely on the presence of others for help and to keep their spirits up.

While we rush through our daily routines, cancer patients fight for one more sunrise, often alone. I prayed before leaving the waiting room that day for God to elevate their spirits and send someone to comfort and support those who could use a companion. In the days that followed, God began to respond to my plea.

God began to place people in my path who needed hope and encouragement—like I needed at the start of my journey. In retrospect, they were probably more helpful to me than I ever was to them. I'll never forget the faith-building experiences that followed over the next few years.

At the beginning of my journey, new to the hospital scene, I recall a woman entering the waiting room on the second day of my radiation treatment. She began staggering as she walked through the doors, falling to the hard floor. I hurried over to assist her in getting up and into the nearest chair. I sat beside her, and we talked while she regained her strength.

She'd been receiving treatment for a while, affecting her physical and mental well-being. In her weakened state, she struggled to comment that my enthusiastic approach to life piqued her interest. At that moment, I remembered how God had strengthened my faith and how it was to be played forward in that moment.

As we sat recuperating together, I put my arm around her and peered into her eyes, saying, "God gave me something that you might can use. The other day, I read the most uplifting verse on faith. It refreshed my mind—*Philippians 1:21-24*. If I live for Christ or die for Christ, it's all good!"

I saw a glimmer of hope return to her tired face as she smiled and thanked me from the bottom of her heart, which I also saw in her eyes. God is good, all the time.

Before we parted ways, we prayed together in an uplifting moment of heavenly gratitude, rekindling her spirit and faith even further. Sometimes, all we need is a simple reminder of God's promises and the presence of His love to restore hope.

As my journey progressed, my faith in God became stronger with each new experience. My friend James started accompanying me to my appointments when I began chemotherapy treatments. During one of the treatment sessions, we met a woman undergoing long-term chemotherapy treatments. Her demeanor indicated she was losing faith in the success of the treatments and possibly her will to live.

James, sensing her need, asked if he could pray with her, and once they finished, I witnessed a spark of optimism in what had become a dim situation. It was a tremendous blessing that James was there to support and encourage her. Seeing someone regain hope to fight such a debilitating illness never gets old—a faith builder from our waymaker, Jesus Christ.

Still another time, James and I were in the pre-op room before my first surgery to remove the tumor. As the nurses connected me to monitors and put on my hospital gown, we noticed a young girl preparing for surgery. She was extremely nervous and was losing her composure. Her parents agreed that we could pray for her, and the fear that held her captive disappeared as God's presence flooded the room, bringing peace and hope.

We may not always be able to see how God works through us, but we must trust His perfect plan and have confidence that He's doing something extraordinary. If we allow God to intervene in our lives, our broken relationships or individual shortcomings will have the perfect catalyst to be mended.

I've often reflected on the life lessons I gained during my cancer struggle, and if God were to ask me if it was worth it all, I'd have to say yes. Throughout it all, his steady presence and goodness restored my hope in life, which had been lost somewhere along the way.

For the first time in quite a while, I believed that whatever obstacles I faced would be overcome. So yes, I would do it all over again to gain the insights that helped chisel away at my inner being to make me a better person with renewed hope.

> *The Lord will accomplish what concerns me; Your lovingkindness, O Lord, is everlasting; Do not forsake the works of Your hands. (Psalm 138:8)*

From God's Perspective:

Love—*always hopes*

> *Lead me by your truth and teach me, for you are the God who saves me. All day long I put my hope in you. (Psalm 25:5)*

From Vice to Virtue:

Whether our relationship is broken, or we want to improve how we handle trying situations, we must believe it will work out in God's perfect timing. If we rush the process, we miss the valuable lessons God wants to teach us, resulting in a temporary fix or, worse, the relationship dissolving. We must wait for the success story that can only come from Him.

> *This is the confidence which we have before Him, that, if we ask anything according to His will, He hears us. And if we know that He hears us in whatever we ask, we know that we have the requests which we have asked from Him. (1 John 5:14–15)*

We progressively become individuals grounded in faith by feeding optimism and starving negativity. Once formed, an optimistic view is maintained by learning to identify the warning signs of prospective hope stealers and eliminate them.

Remember, the attitude we feed—wins.

Here are some characteristics of a cynical person:

- Pessimistic personality

- Unmotivated

- Reluctant toward changes

- Focuses on past failures

Pessimistic personality:

Would you define yourself as a pessimist or a realist? The realist is the problem solver who considers all logical factors to achieve the best solution to a problem or circumstance. Pessimists, on the other hand, argue why any reasonable answer could fail or why our efforts should be abandoned. Most of us probably consider ourselves realists, but is that really who we are?

The perspectives we allow to govern our thoughts can often determine the outcome of situations. If we have the mindset that we'll fail, we unconsciously start preparing for failure. However, if we remain optimistic, we'll be prepared to work through any obstacles that might impede our success.

Controlling how our minds navigate situations is half the battle—negativity drains our determination, whereas optimism fuels motivation. From a positive outlook, even if we fail, we still win because we gain experience; however, if we never try, we gain nothing. A dash of optimism, a sprinkle of motivation, an ounce of faith, and a pinch of experience perfectly season the recipe for s uccess.

> *For there is hope for a tree, when it is cut down, that it will sprout again, and its shoots will not fail. Though its roots grow old in the ground and its stump dies in the dry soil, at the scent of water it*

> *will flourish and put forth sprigs like a plant.* (Job 14:7-9)

Unmotivated:

Most of us have a driving force that propels us forward, such as a better lifestyle for our family, financial security, or hopes of career success. However, without motivation, no amount of hope will help us change or achieve anything. Being unmotivated is like planning a trip in a vehicle without gas—the journey will be delayed till we fill up.

In order for us to fill up our determination gas tank, we must discover what causes our lack of passion. We begin by asking ourselves a few simple "Do we" questions:

- Do we consider ourselves pessimists or optimists?
- Do we feel our daily routine is overwhelming us?
- Do we give up when obstacles become challenging?
- Do we feel our spouse supports us with encouragement to obtain goals?
- Do we regard ourselves as unmotivated or determined, and if so, why?
- Do we contribute our time and effort to achieve the goals that seem out of our reach?

Our first point of change is understanding that we should readily offer encouragement when our spouse is in need. And let's be clear—it's what both partners should be doing regularly to promote the individual and the relationship. Encouragement from a spouse is a godly characteristic and a powerful hope builder that can change the most hopeless of circumstances. It's amazing what the words of someone we love can do to awaken our lack of motivation.

> *and let's consider how to encourage one another in love and good deeds, not abandoning our own meeting together, as is the habit of some people, but encouraging one another; and all the more as you see the day drawing near. (Hebrews 10:24–25)*

Plucking the "Weeds" of Hope:

Past generations acquired knowledge through reading, collaborating, writing down their thoughts, and transacting most of their business using paper documents. As the computer era emerged, pencil and paper became progressively outdated, and Google became the go-to resource for advice and information.

Most people from previous eras found the learning curve and lack of human interaction brought about by the new digital era unwelcome. Going into town to pay bills and socializing with the clerks and other customers was an enjoyable and anticipated experience for my parents. They argued that human socialization declined as humanity evolved in the digital age.

At the time, I couldn't comprehend what I perceived as flawed reasoning. I was baffled as to why they couldn't see how much effort and time it would save, allowing them to enjoy other aspects of life. The more I pressed the subject, the more they resisted until I gave up trying to convert them to my way of thinking. Years and many life experiences later, I recognized the wisdom in their resistance.

My parents were part of a generation that had endured the Second World War and the Great Depression when people relied on one another instead of technological innovations. It was a time when, rather than sending someone a quick text, they physically went to spend time consoling those suffering tragedy—a value not as common today.

The power of human touch and engaging in non-digital conversations that encourage and soothe our emotional suffering are mercilessly omitted by modern technology. As we age and life slows down, it's clear why past generations labored so hard to keep the "weeds" out of their cherished way of life, which valued the love and presence of people.

It's all too easy to send that quick text to someone who could use our presence as they struggle through life's challenges. My past is plagued with strained relationships where I failed to be there in physical form. Trust me, from experience, broken connections will not be repaired in our absence.

We must remember that we only get so many do-overs until a relationship is beyond repair. We must always safeguard against anything that reduces our human interaction. We must spend time—plucking the weeds.

> *Let your eyes look directly ahead and let your gaze be fixed straight in front of you. Watch the path of your feet and all your ways will be established. (Proverbs 4:25–26)*

Reluctant Toward Changes:

While avoiding anything that can undermine our hope, we must equally be willing to navigate necessary and inevitable changes proactively. While concerns about the initial adjustments are understandable, the cynical person's questions are geared toward finding fault to stop the changes from happening.

Rather than waiting to see if the changes could improve the process, they focus solely on how it will fail. The most effective way to counteract doubt is to be patient and empathetic while initiating small steps toward the goal. We must provide the confidence that the cynic lacks during the transitions.

> *If the Lord had not been my help, my soul would soon*

> *have dwelt in the abode of silence. If I should say, "My foot has slipped," Your lovingkindness, O Lord, will hold me up. When my anxious thoughts multiply within me, Your consolations delight my soul. (Psalm 94:17-19)*

Focuses on Past Failures:

Have you ever wondered why some people are at ease commenting about their past but avoid talking about their future? For the cynical person, the past may hold unpleasant memories and regrets, but it's also familiarity with no surprises. From their perspective, it's an atmosphere of comfort.

A reluctance to focus on the future often stems from a fear of change. Sometimes, we may be afraid of stepping outside our comfort zone, fearing a terrible experience will happen again. For example, a couple who recently lost their home in a fire highlights the difference between skeptical and optimistic viewpoints.

The husband wants to stay in the same neighborhood, but his wife doesn't want to be constantly reminded of their devastating loss. He tries to ease her feelings by suggesting to build their long-discussed dream home in the same neighborhood. In this way, they would remain within the support of their friends and enable their children to attend the same accredited school. It would offer familiar support for everyone.

The plan seems logical to the optimist. However, re-establishing their life in the same location is a terrifying reminder for the wary wife. She can only think of the possibility that if they rebuild, another fire may destroy their new home. In her apprehension, she overlooks all the benefits her current community offers to the family dynamics.

Understandably, her fears stem from the devastating event she experienced and contribute to her negative outlook. So, how can we reason with a skeptical person? As always, we affirm their feelings, demonstrating that we're sensitive to their concerns and that their voices matter.

We must try to transform each fear into a source of hope, reassuring them that we'll address any problems that arise together. If we cannot reach a compromise, we must accept that their fears are real and that forcing change could only serve to worsen the problem. Make the solution one of hope for everyone as we let love and patience guide the way.

> *constantly bearing in mind your work of faith and labor of love and steadfastness of hope in the Lord Jesus Christ in the presence of our God and Father. (1 Thessalonians 1:3)*

Final Thoughts:

Faith is like a muscle. It strengthens when exercised but weakens when not used. When things in our lives are out of sync, or we cannot fix what is broken, we must believe that God is working behind the scenes to repair what is beyond our means. Through this unconditional confidence in God, we develop our faith and will live without a constant fear of the unknown.

Relationships work the same way. We must learn to put our trust in one another and to believe that with dedicated effort, the perfect outcome is just around the corner. In time, the challenges we face as individuals and in our relationships will be overcome, knowing that God is on our side and wants what's best for us.

Resolving problems without hope and an uncompromised faith in God compares to trying to row up a waterfall in a rowboat. It's not going to happen. For a successful relationship, we must eliminate anything that has the potential to undermine our hope. We must be steadfast in eradicating the "weeds" that can swiftly develop and undermine the hope within our relationships. Nothing is too broken or impossible for God.

> *And looking at them, Jesus said to them, "With people this is impossible, but with God all things are possible." (Matthew 19:26)*

If we don't have faith in God or others, we won't look for a reason for a change to happen—we'll give up or stop trying. God has patience with us, and we must have patience with one another.

But if we hope for what we do not see, through perseverance we wait eagerly for it. (Romans 8:25)

Strategy for Success:

- Remove the things that consistently sap our hope.

- Optimistic people solve problems by believing that every problem has a solution.

- A pessimistic attitude rarely leads to a solution and only serves to impede results or progress.

- Remove the mindset, "It will fail."

- Set goals. When we achieve our objectives—we strengthen our faith in God.

- Stop reliving the past. Let the goals we set pave the way for embracing the future.

- Learn the skills needed to achieve goals. Don't be afraid of new things.

Related Scripture:

- *Proverbs 3:3–4*
- *Hebrews 11:1*
- *Matthew 17:20*
- *Matthew 21:22*
- *Mark 9:23*

Let God Fight the Battle:

Loving Father,
We thank You for the countless blessings You graciously bestow upon us.
Father, we pray for the courage to persevere with renewed hope as we place our total trust in You.
May we always have the eyes of hope and the heart of faith as Your flawless plan unfolds.
Father, grant us victory in times of adversity and temptation.
We seek these things in Jesus' holy name,
Amen.

Chapter Fourteen

WE'RE UNDER ATTACK

"If we're obedient to God's divine authority while wearing God's Armor, we've won the battle before it begins."

An age-old spiritual war is going on, and we're in the middle of the battle. God and Satan are contending for our allegiance, leaving us faced with the most crucial decision of our lives. Either we commit to serve God and His truth or allow Satan to deceive us, which leads to eternal death and separation from God.

How did we end up in a spiritual war? What does it have to do with us, and why does it matter so much? Our story starts to unfold in Genesis, the Bible's first book.

In the beginning, God created the first humans, Adam and Eve, and placed them in the Garden of Eden. He then designed marriage to connect Adam and Eve—the first love story. Driven by his enmity for humanity, Satan devises a cunning plot to create havoc and sabotage the relationship God has just established between the first humans.

Here's how it all unfolds. In the middle of the garden stood two trees. The first was the Tree of Life, which offered an everlasting existence; the second was the Tree of Knowledge of Good and Evil, ensuring eternal death. Adam and Eve could eat from any of the garden's fruits, but only one was forbidden—the Tree of Knowledge of Good and Evil.

> *The LORD God commanded the man, saying, "From any tree of the garden you may freely eat; but from the tree of the knowledge of good and evil you shall not eat, for on the day that you eat from it you will certainly die." (Genesis 2:16–17)*

By God putting the Tree of Knowledge of Good and Evil in the garden, He gave humanity the ability to make choices—free will. Satan took advantage of this liberty by luring Eve to eat from the Tree of Knowledge of Good and Evil, defying God.

Eve's disobedience in eating the forbidden fruit began our spiritual battle and introduced sin into the perfect paradise. From that point forward, Satan forever tempts us into disobeying God and destroying our relationships. He's a crafty and devious adversary—if we choose to worship God, we must be vigilant and learn Satan's destructive strategies.

> *But I am afraid that, as the serpent deceived Eve by his craftiness, your minds will be led astray from the simplicity and purity of devotion to Christ. (2 Corinthians 11:3)*

Satan's Devious Ways of Temptation:

Satan will tempt us using several devious methods, but his favorite approach is to twist Scripture to suit his purposes. When Satan enticed Eve to eat from the Tree of Knowledge of Good and Evil, he led her to question what God had told her. In the following verse, notice how Satan has us question our understanding of God's Word by twisting and creating doubt:

> *Now the serpent was more cunning than any animal of the field which the LORD God had made. And he said to the woman, "Has God really said, You shall not eat from any tree of the garden?" The woman said to the serpent, "From the fruit of the trees of the garden we may eat; but from the fruit of the*

> *tree which is in the middle of the garden, God has said, You shall not eat from it or touch it, or you will die." The serpent said to the woman, "You certainly will not die! For God knows that on the day you eat from it your eyes will be opened, and you will become like God, knowing good and evil." (Genesis 3:1-5)*

Satan exploits the desire to be like God to deceive Eve, anticipating her to crave the same weakness that led to his eternal downfall. The temptation worked—she ate from the forbidden tree, persuading Adam to follow suit. This could very well be where the adage, "Misery loves company," originated.

Two things we must remember about Satan: he can outwit the most educated and brightest theologians and will try to seduce us anytime the opportunity presents itself. He doesn't deny God's Word but instead exploits it to undermine our faith in God's will.

Satan tempted Jesus in three primary areas during the temptation of Christ, which he continues to use with us today:

- Hedonism (pleasing ourselves)

- Egoism (focused on personal greatness)

- Materialism (love of possessions)

As Satan did with Eve, he'll figure out our fleshly desires and use them to draw us into sin during our weak moments. He's a formidable adversary who seeks every opportunity to strike when we're most vulnerable. In today's world, where people desire worldly pleasures more than ever, it's easier for Satan to infiltrate our lives and cause mayhem.

> *Be of sober spirit, be on the alert. Your adversary, the devil, prowls around like a roaring lion, seeking someone to devour. But resist him, firm in your faith, knowing that the same experiences of suffering are being accomplished by your brethren who are in the world. (1 Peter 5:8–9)*

Don't Make Satan's Job Easier:

One of the most effective means of exposing ourselves to potential temptations is through television, the brain drainer. Almost everyone on the planet watches TV to some extent, making it an effortless catalyst for Satan's work. Modern entertainment freely exposes audiences to extreme adult graphics exploitation that was once restricted to viewers over eighteen.

Television offers a buffet of nudity, sex, drugs, violence, profanity, pedophilia, and a diverse criminal education. It's also habit forming, resulting in social isolation, wasting valuable time, causing depression and anxiety, and contributing to health concerns. I'm sure more negative impacting aspects could be listed, but those came to mind.

Today's programs have everything Satan loves for us to indoctrinate our minds *(Hedonism, Egoism, Materialism)*. With the press of a button, we can view everything Scripture says to avoid. Constant exposure to worldly things can weaken our spirits and lead to temptation, opening the door for spiritual attacks.

Watching too much television can also cause us to lose focus on what's important. I used to rush home, eat dinner, shower, and spend the evening watching the screen and relaxing—a victory for Satan. Thankfully, I began to realize that my evening ritual was driving me to overlook my obligations and goals—a victory for God.

Not only was I slacking on my tasks, but I was also exposing my mind to unwholesome things that could inadvertently indoctrinate my thoughts. A previously stated Scripture reveals the fleshly lures that we should avoid if seeking to attain and preserve a healthy perspective on life:

> *Now the deeds of the flesh are evident, which are: sexual immorality, impurity, indecent behavior, idolatry, witchcraft, hostilities, strife, jealousy, outbursts of anger,*

> *selfish ambition, dissensions, factions, envy, drunkenness, carousing, and things like these, of which I forewarn you, just as I have forewarned you, that those who practice such things will not inherit the kingdom of God. (Galatians 5:19–21)*

Everything we see on television occurs in reality and can be a source of temptation. In the above passage, what undesirable behaviors are we not exposing our minds to by watching most of the channels in today's programming? We must break the habit of exposing ourselves to seduction by willingly opening the door.

We may argue that we only watch wholesome, educational, uplifting, and positive shows. That's great if we only view such programs—we've made precautions to shield our minds from harmful stimuli. However, it remains a vice if our time watching the screen prevents us from achieving our goals or neglects our relationships.

I'm not suggesting we never watch television. It can be a fantastic source of relaxation and a terrific educational tool if used in moderation and filtered to prevent unfavorable ideas and images.

> *I will set no worthless thing before my eyes; I hate the work of those who fall away;*

> *it shall not fasten its grip on*
> *me. (Psalm 101:3)*

How Do We Fight Satan's Attacks?:

In the same way that Satan deceived Eve into undermining God's design for humanity, he continues seeking to destroy anything good in our lives. Satan will continuously pursue instances where he believes we'll fail the spiritual onslaught. He loves to attack when:

- He perceives God is preparing us for something good.

- When we complete an act that serves God's kingdom or purpose.

- When we're most vulnerable. *(alone, afraid, weak, grieving, hungry, sinful...)*

- Attacks in weak moments using a person we trust. *(spouse, family, friend, coworker...)*

- When we think the spiritual attack is finished. *(catches us off guard by attacking again)*

Awareness is our foremost shield of protection against being a victim of his crafty efforts of attack. Remember, he despises God's will and hates us out of jealousy of God's love for us—he doesn't want us to succeed. Therefore, we can anticipate an attack when attempting to mend a strained connection or being united.

His attack could be when we recognize we're to blame, and he attempts to convince us that it's our spouse's fault. It could also be when we aren't at fault, and he doesn't want us to extend forgiveness, yet another way to keep the relationship unreconciled. Like a predator attacking the weak, he'll lash out from all possible angles.

The good news is that God has given us the tools to fight Satan's attacks. God conveys His faithfulness and assures us that He's ready to help us in our time of need.

> *Do not fear, for I am with you; Do not anxiously look about you, for I am your God. I will strengthen you, surely I will help you, surely I will uphold you with My righteous right hand. (Isaiah 41:10)*

In my darkest and weakest moments, I've read the verse above several times to absorb and reflect on its encouragement and hope. We strengthen ourselves for battle by remaining faithful to God's will and devoted to Him as victory over the enemy is won.

Spiritual attacks are often successful when we favor earthly pleasures or worldly solutions over God during times of need. For example, if we quarrel with our spouse and then down a bottle of booze to drown our sorrows. Instead of trusting God to help us work it out, we make it worse by allowing temptation into our lives. What if intoxication caused harm to ourselves or others, adding to our existing relationship problems?

We must always put our trust in an eternal God, not the pleasures of a failing world. He has gracefully provided us with a form of protection against Satan and his diabolical attacks—the divine Armor of God.

> *Finally, be strong in the Lord and in the strength of His might. Put on the full armor of God, so that you will be able to stand firm against the schemes of the devil. For our struggle is not against flesh and blood, but against the rulers, against the powers, against the world forces of this darkness, against the spiritual forces of wickedness in the heavenly places. Therefore, take up the full armor of God, so that you will be able to resist in the evil day, and having done everything, to stand firm. Stand firm therefore, having girded your loins with truth, and having put on the breastplate of righteousness, and having*

> *shod your feet with the preparation of the gospel of peace; in addition to all, taking up the shield of faith with which you will be able to extinguish all the flaming arrows of the evil one. And take the helmet of salvation, and the sword of the Spirit, which is the word of God. (Ephesians 6:10–17)*

Let's dissect each section of this passage to understand each piece of the armor.

<u>having girded your loins with truth</u>- God's Word contains the truth. Jesus defeated Satan's temptations by quoting God's Word. To effectively present the truth, we must strengthen our knowledge of Scripture.

> *Truthful lips will be established forever, but a lying tongue is only for a moment. (Proverbs 12:19)*

<u>put on the breastplate of righteousness</u>- The breastplate of a warrior protects the vital organs, such as the heart, which seeds our emotions. Satan cannot influence our hearts to make bad decisions if we obey God's Word and do what pleases Him.

> *I have treasured Your word in my heart, So that I may not sin against You. (Psalm 119:11)*

<u>having shod your feet with the preparation of the gospel of peace</u>- Satan will want to steal the peace and contentment that Jesus' sacrifice on the cross has brought us. Our joy of salvation should be spread to others, letting them know the source of our serenity is God. In doing so, we remain planted on a foundation of peace and truth.

> *The steadfast of mind You will keep in perfect peace, because he trusts in You. Trust in the Lord forever, for in God the Lord, we have an everlasting rock. (Isaiah 26:3–4)*

<u>taking up the shield of faith</u>- We wield the shield of faith by believing God knows what's best for us and waiting patiently for it to happen. We must never lose confidence in God's ability to provide and to give us victory in battle. As our faith in God grows, so does our ability to repel attacks.

We must never let our guard down and allow Satan to control our minds and hearts. If we do, he will try to destroy our faith in God's capacity to win the battles and, eventually, the war.

> *Trust in the Lord with all your heart and do not lean on your own understanding. In all your ways acknowledge Him, and He will make your paths straight. (Proverbs 3:5–6)*

<u>take the helmet of salvation</u>- The helmet of salvation shields our minds from worldly thoughts and Satan's lies. We must always defend the truth of Jesus dying on the cross to give us access to God and to atone for our sins—our salvation. Satan will try to convince us that Jesus' sacrifice hasn't saved us from our sins and was a wasted effort.

> *And do not be conformed to this world, but be transformed by the renewing of your mind, so that you may prove what the will of God is, that which is good and acceptable and perfect. (Romans 12:2)*

<u>sword of the Spirit, which is the Word of God</u>- An unhealthy body cannot easily defend itself against physical assault. Likewise, we must feed our minds with God's Word daily to grow spiritually stronger. By enhancing our minds with truth, we can deflect spiritual attacks with the sword of the Spirit.

Notice in the Scripture below how Jesus used this divine method to deflect Satan during the temptations of Christ.

> *But He answered and said,*
> *It is written, man shall not*
> *live on bread alone, but*
> *on every word that proceeds*
> *out of the mouth of God.*
> *(Matthew 4:4)*

To defend ourselves against spiritual attacks, we must practice and develop the virtues of *1 Corinthians 13:4-8*, which produces the fruits of the Spirit. By doing so, we strengthen God's armor to defend ourselves against spiritual attacks. As we mature spiritually, our relationships will develop resilience to survive the seasons of life.

God's Free Gift to Us:

The attributes of love we've examined will undoubtedly help us grow as individuals and contribute to the success of our relationships. However, without Jesus completing the cord of three in our marriages, we'll struggle to build an everlasting and resilient foundation of hope. *(Ecclesiastes 4:12)*

Jesus is the light that guides us in the darkness and becomes the strength we lack when we feel we're unable to endure. When the storms of life come, and they will, we need a savior who can be our beacon of hope, preventing us from sinking into the depths.

Only through Jesus' love and sacrifice on the cross can we discover true happiness in ourselves and with others. Jesus severed every yoke that bound us to a life of despair and separation from God.

Through Jesus, we find peace beyond our comprehension.

> *And the peace of God, which surpasses all comprehension, will guard your hearts and minds in Christ Jesus. (Philippians 4:7)*

Choosing God as a partner in our personal lives and marriages will be a turning point—He can fix what we cannot.

So, how do we allow God into our lives? It's simple—we confess that our lives are misguided and not pleasing to Him and that we need His mercy and grace to forgive us of our sins.

We must acknowledge that Jesus died for our sins and rose again as our savior. Seeking God with a sincere heart, turning from our old sinful ways, and confessing Jesus as Lord begins our new path of peace, hope, and joy in life.

> *if you confess with your mouth Jesus as Lord, and believe in your heart that God raised Him from the dead,*

> *you will be saved; for with the heart a person believes, resulting in righteousness, and with the mouth he confesses, resulting in salvation. (Romans 10:9–10)*

What Should I Do Now That I've Accepted Jesus?

Begin by reading the Bible daily as it feeds our spirit and strengthens our defenses against spiritual attacks. The Bible is God's living Word and speaks to us at various times when we need to hear a specific message.

Scripture is alive and breathing and has an answer for every situation we may face. I've read the Bible multiple times and always learn something new, often when faced with a problem. God loves to show up and connect and reassure us in our moments of need.

Next, choose a church where you can be fed biblical truth and grow spiritually. Participate in church activities and get to know the people who attend. When needed, church members can be a powerful source of spiritual encouragement and stability as we grow in Christ. After you've met the members, look for a mentor with whom you can connect and may share a common bond. They can help you stay on course as you develop as a new Christian.

You now have a relationship with God, and He wants to spend time with you. Talk to Him daily by establishing a prayer routine to convey your needs and discover His will for your new life. When we pray, consider it a relaxed conversation with a friend rather than a formal ritual with a stranger. As we openly approach God, our interactions with Him will become one of Father and child.

As we strengthen our spiritual lives, we weaken Satan's grip. We must remember that Satan has no power over us unless we give him access to our lives. We only leave an open door when we allow him unrestricted entry by returning to the old ways that failed us.

> *This means that anyone who belongs to Christ has become a new person. The old life is gone; a new life has begun! (2 Corinthians 5:17)*

Our relationships will improve as we modify our lifestyles. It will not happen overnight; we'll have obstacles and setbacks, but we must keep the faith. What matters is that we continue developing into the individuals God and our partners want and deserve. It's through the love of God and the saving grace of Jesus we have hope.

Chapter Fifteen
Never Surrender

"The tiny ant can teach us enormous lessons about never giving up."

Ants have long fascinated me with how they race around and carry out their never-ending endeavors. Without an ant's comprehension, their activities are sometimes obvious as they gather and deliver resources to their mound. At other times, it just seems to be a mindless frenzy of rushing around that appears to be a waste of energy.

The more I observe the tiny ant's seemingly crazy antics, the more I notice one thing that sticks out—their tolerance for one another. It's intriguing to watch an ant crawl up a blade of grass where another ant obstructed its path, understand the situation, and, without hesitation, redirect its route.

Another observation, regardless of how often their mound is destroyed by nature or foe, the colony always works together to make repairs. They don't waste time dwelling on what happened or assigning blame—they only seek to restore the home that shields them from the elements. Could we learn anything from the tiny ant?

Whatever life throws at them, the tiny ants ignore the barriers and focus on the intended objective. What if we applied the same perseverance, forgiveness, and devotion in our relationships as the ant employs to survive? Would it alleviate some of the problems we may face in our current relationship? Would it help us navigate life's challenging moments in unity and without animosity? We could learn much from the tiny ant that focuses on the solution rather than the problem.

The Four Components of Perseverance:

Like the weather, relationships move through seasons of change and transformation, bringing us times of joy and sadness that begin and end. Four relational components will influence our thoughts, words, and actions during these continual changes. To navigate the seasons of life successfully, we need to practice:

- Removal of pride
- Unyielding patience
- Self-control
- Forgiveness

Love Is Not Proud: (Removal of Pride)

The absence of pride allows the other three essential elements to function properly. Pride is the most powerful vice that can block our progress in whatever we try to achieve. Here are some of my old "couldn't be me" justifications for failed relationships:

- <u>They don't know how to love.</u> –Is it conceivable that we don't understand how to respond to love?

- <u>They lack relationship skills</u>. –I've thought this about my partner with flared emotions and a stiffened face while continuously ranting about their lack of relational skills.

- <u>They never think it's their fault.</u> –Do we accept responsibility or make a habit of blaming others?

- <u>They say unkind things to me.</u> –When we speak love with salt, we all must be careful not to overseason.

> *There is one who speaks rashly like the thrusts of a sword, But the tongue of the wise brings healing. (Proverbs 12:18)*

- <u>They make life all about themselves.</u> –Life is like a pie—everyone should get a piece to enjoy the sweetness. Do we ever ask our partners what they want to do, or do they consent to whatever is on the agenda? Is it possible that the person who goes with the flow is more humbly concerned with our happiness than their own?

> *Don't look out only for your own interests, but take an interest in others, too. (Philippians 2:4)*

- <u>They don't support anything I do.</u> –This emotion tends to form when the other person doesn't feel equally supported. Do we acknowledge or make a sincere attempt to encourage or participate in our partner's ambitions or endeavors?

> *Can two people walk together without agreeing on the direction? (Amos 3:3)*

- <u>They never help me do chores.</u> –Perhaps we should be more aware of the chores they do that we overlook.

As you can see from my past illogical reasoning, pride prevented me from recognizing how much I was at fault for my previous relationship breakdowns. The delusion of pride preys on our humility, which enables us to identify, accept, and humbly ask forgiveness as we correct our shortcomings.

We'll never see a change in ourselves or our relationships if we allow pride to hide our imperfections. Deflection or unfairly blaming our partners will continue, and the relationship will suffer. As we grow in humility, we remove pride.

Love Is Patient: (Unyielding Patience)

Patience, the foundation of the relationship, is the primary catalyst for building and maintaining the other love virtues. It fosters and increases self-control, which aids in removing pride and allows us to be more proactive rather than reactive. A forgiving heart is the virtuous embodiment and ultimate fruit of patience.

Love Is Not Easily Angered: (Self-control)

In the chapter, *Humble Pride*, we talked about how "self" words are egotistical and should be removed from our vocabulary. Self-control is the exception to the rule. Without it, our destructive emotions will dominate our reactions, exacerbating the situation or sabotaging any progress in resolving an issue.

When navigating adversity, we must remember to safeguard our relationship from ourselves. Remember, we use the TWA system to help ensure our thoughts, words, and actions are constructive and supportive of a situation. Keep the focus on the solution and not the problem.

> *Like a city that is broken into and without walls is a man who has no control over his spirit. (Proverbs 25:28)*

Love Keeps No Record of Wrongs: (Forgiveness)

Every day gives us a fresh start—if we choose. We can forgive yesterday's conflict or allow it to fester. When it's difficult to forgive, the depth of our love and commitment are tested.

Remember, love doesn't keep records of wrongs. When we tell someone we can't dismiss an offense, we put conditions on our relationship. Jesus defines the true meaning of unconditional love in His teachings.

> *But I say to you, love your enemies and pray for those who persecute you, so that you may be sons of your Father who is in heaven; for He causes His sun to rise on the evil and the good, and sends rain on the righteous and the unrighteous. For if you love those who love you, what reward do you have? Do not even the tax collectors do the same? (Matthew 5:44–46)*

On my desk, I have a 4"x 8" glass container filled with sand. On top of the sand is a Bible with two very distinct stones lying on the cover. A rough stone represents me, and a smooth stone symbolizes Shelah. While the rocks are equal in size, they differ in texture and composition.

Like the stones, Shelah and I are different. Although we're married and becoming one via sanctification, we remain individuals created in God's image and by His design. The container reminds me that while we all share certain human traits, we have distinctive characteristics, qualities, and shortcomings that contribute to our uniqueness. Not wrong—just different.

God created us to complement and help one another, not compete. The master instructor, Jesus, inspired the stone display: Before pointing out Shelah's weaknesses, I must examine myself first.

> *But when they persisted in asking Him, He straightened up, and said to them, "He who is without sin among you, let him be the first to throw a stone at her." (John 8:7)*

Persevering Through the Seasons:

As we understand that we make mistakes as individuals, we must also accept that the relationship will go through seasons—they're a natural part of life. The changes in life we go through together either make us stronger or more distant as a couple. They put us to the test, making us realize how vulnerable our humanity is and our need to be supportive partners. Be at peace, God will walk through the storms with us.

> *Like a bad tooth and an unsteady foot is confidence in a faithless man in time of trouble. (Proverbs 29:19)*

When we build our relationships according to *God's Love Manual*, the Bible, we build on the rock of ages. On this solid foundation, we find truth and can put our faith in the One who existed before time and can fix what we can't—never surrender.

God is love, and love never fails. He can make a way where all seems lost if we only have faith. If we follow His guidance, we'll establish a relationship that's fulfilling in every way and continues to bring us endless happiness.

> *Therefore everyone who hears these words of Mine and acts on them, may be compared to a wise man who built his house on the rock. And the rain fell, and the floods came, and the winds blew and slammed against that house; and yet it did not fall, for it had been founded on the rock. Everyone who hears*

> *these words of Mine and does not act on them, will be like a foolish man who built his house on the sand. The rain fell, and the floods came, and the winds blew and slammed against that house; and it fell—and great was its fall. (Matthew 7:24-27)*

May your relationship be blessed with abundant love that will satisfy all your desires and expectations. As the closeness with your spouse increases, never forget what God has done in your relationship. Each morning, thank Him for the love that surrounds and holds your heart as you walk through this life together.

As you reflect on the love in your heart, I hope you return the blessings of His teachings in good measure to others in their relational struggles. May the God of peace and love guide your ways—Love never fails!

> *If I can stop one heart from breaking, I shall not live in vain; If I can ease one life the aching, or cool one pain, or help one fainting robin unto his nest again, I shall not live in vain. -Emily Dickinson*

Thank you for allowing me to share some of my most memorable moments of relational successes and failures. If the messages in *God's Love Manual: A How-to Guide for Building Successful Relationships* have touched your heart or impacted your life, I'd love to hear from you and celebrate the victory. May God bless and show grace in all you do.

www.johnkslater.com

I want to thank you so much for taking the time to read

GOD'S LOVE MANUAL

A How-to Guide for Building Successful Relationships

I hope it has touched your heart in some way that draws you closer to God. If you enjoyed reading it, I would love it if you could leave a review on a retailer's site or Goodreads (you don't have to have bought a book there to leave a review)."

AVAILABLE ONLINE NOW
AT YOUR FAVORITE BOOK STORE OR WWW.JOHNKSLATER.COM

THE DELIBERATE CHRISTIAN:

A DISCIPLESHIP GUIDE FOR THE NEW BELIEVER

**EVERY DESTINATION HAS A BEGINNING.
EMBARK ON YOUR SPIRITUAL JOURNEY NOW!**

www.ingramcontent.com/pod-product-compliance
Lightning Source LLC
LaVergne TN
LVHW051044080426
835508LV00019B/1689